T0072580

The Rivers Join

The Story Of A Family

NICHOLAS CRICKHOWELL

Note for Librarians: A cataloguing record for this book is available from Library and Archives Canada at www.collectionscanada.ca/amicus/index-e.html

Printed in Victoria, BC, Canada.

ISBN: 978-1-4251-9142-9 (sc)

Our mission is to efficiently provide the world's finest, most comprehensive book publishing service, enabling every author to experience success. To find out how to publish your book, your way, and have it available worldwide, visit us online at www.trafford.com

Trafford rev. 11/23/2009

 www.trafford.com

North America & international
toll-free: 1 888 232 4444 (USA & Canada)
phone: 250 383 6864 ♦ fax: 812 355 4082

Contents

Royal Artillery plays an heroic role in Marlborough's wars. We hear about the Healings. Jacobus van Rhenen arrives in South Africa. Our Huguenot ancestors arrive in Ireland (after extraordinary adventures) and Nathaniel Wallich is born in Copenhagen. We learn for the first time about the Godbys.

THE RIVERS

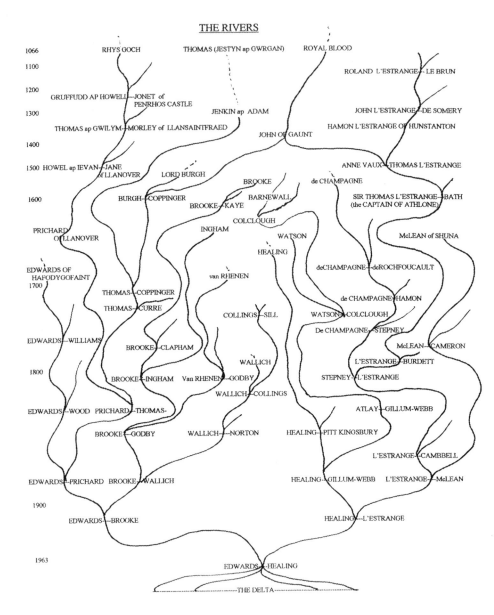

1066	RHYS GOCH THOMAS (JESTYN ap GWRGAN) ROYAL BLOOD
1100	ROLAND L'ESTRANGE──LE BRUN
1200	GRUFFUDD AP HOWELL──JONET of
	PENRHOS CASTLE
1300	JENKIN ap ADAM JOHN L'ESTRANGE──DE SOMERY
	THOMAS ap GWILYM──MORLEY of LLANSAINTFRAED HAMON L'ESTRANGE OF HUNSTANTON
1400	JOHN OF GAUNT
1500 HOWEL ap IEVAN──JANE	ANNE VAUX──THOMAS L'ESTRANGE
	of LLANOVER LORD BURGH de CHAMPAGNE
	BROOKE
1600	BURGH──COPPINGER BARNEWALL SIR THOMAS L'ESTRANGE──BATH
	BROOKE──KAYE (the CAPTAIN OF ATHLONE)
	COLCLOUGH
	PRICHARD INGHAM WATSON McLEAN of SHUNA
	of LLANOVER HEALING
	EDWARDS OF deCHAMPAGNE──deROCHFOUCAULT
	HAFODYGOFAINT van RHENEN
1700	de CHAMPAGNE──HAMON
	THOMAS──COPPINGER
	THOMAS──CURRE COLLINGS──SILL WATSON──COLCLOUGH
	De CHAMPAGNE──STEPNEY
	EDWARDS──WILLIAMS McLEAN──CAMERON
	BROOKE──CLAPHAM WALLICH L'ESTRANGE──BURDETT
1800	STEPNEY──L'ESTRANGE
	BROOKE──INGHAM Van RHENEN──GODBY
	WALLICH──COLLINGS
	EDWARDS──WOOD PRICHARD──THOMAS── ATLAY──GILLUM-WEBB
	BROOKE──GODBY WALLICH──NORTON HEALING──PITT KINGSBURY
	L'ESTRANGE──CAMBBELL
	EDWARDS──PRICHARD BROOKE──WALLICH HEALING──GILLUM-WEBB L'ESTRANGE──McLEAN
1900	EDWARDS──BROOKE HEALING──L'ESTRANGE
1963	EDWARDS──HEALING
	─────THE DELTA─────

Preface.

In writing the story of the family there is a problem about names, particularly with the L'Estranges. In the eight hundred years covered by this history the form of the name has changed from its original Norman French. In order to be consistent I have used the form L'Estrange except when I am quoting from a passage in which another form is used. Again there are other names where we find variations of use. Hamon and Hamo is one such case; but I have used Hamon throughout. Hawyse is sometimes spelt Hawise; I have stuck to the former. I prefer McLean to MacLean. I am less consistent about my wife's name, Ankaret, in that more often than not I use the name by which most people refer to her, Ann. In the sections concerning Wales I have used the Welsh spelling of names and places, even when the English form such as David or Glendower may be more familiar to some of my readers.

I owe a huge debt to the late Winston Guthrie Jones Q.C. whose thoroughly researched paper *The Family of L'Estrange and the Conquest of Wales*, completed in 1987 and dedicated to his wife Janet and her children Guy and Fiona L'Estrange, provided much of the material on which the first three chapters are based. I have also incorporated facts and judgements obtained from more recently published works, including books by R. R. Davies and the magisterial life of Llywelyn ap Gruffydd by J. Beverley Smith. I am equally indebted to Petra Coffey, wife of Ann's cousin Manus, for the information about the family's Huguenot forebears and for some useful thoughts about George Burdett L'Estrange. Winston Guthrie Jones provided his own list of acknowledgements which I only repeat where I have made direct reference to them myself. Much of the detailed history of the L'Estranges before 1310 can be found in *The Le Strange Records AD1100-1310* by Hamon Le Strange. Cord Oestmann's *Lordship and Community* added useful detail. Among the most important studies of the Welsh Wars to which I have referred are: *The Thirteenth Century* by Sir Maurice Powicke, *The Age of Conquest Wales 1063-1415* by R. R. Davies, together with the *Conquest Coexistence and Change 1063-1415* and *The revolt of Owain Glyn Dŵr*. John Davies covers much of the ground in *A History of Wales; and The Welsh Wars of Edward I* by J. E Morris remains an important source, particularly of military information. I quote from *A History of the Crusades* by Stephen Runciman.

When I come to the Irish side of the L'Estrange family there are references to *The Calendar of the Patent Rolls Ireland* of the period of Henry VIII and Elizabeth I; There are substantial exracts from *The Recollections of Sir George L'Estrange* and from *The Wexford Rising* by Charles Dickson; I have used *Memoirs of the Different Rebellions in Ireland* by Sir Richard Musgrave, Bart.; *A New History of Ireland* by R. B. Mc Dowell; and *A History of Ireland in the 18th Century* by W. E. H. Lecky. I have also taken material from *The Irish Country House* by Peter Somerville-Large and *Extraneous News,* the Journal of the Le Strange Society (Mr Neal Wood).

Material on the Huguenots comes from two papers by Thomas Philip Le Fanu in *The Proceedings of The Huguenot Society, Vol. VIII, Nos 5 and 6. 1928; Marie de la Rochefoncauld de Champagné and her Escape from France in 1687,* and *The Children of Marie de la Rochefoncauld de Champagné.*

Information about Colonel Jonas Watson, the first Lieutenant-Colonel of the Royal Artillery, came from family records and The Royal Artillery Historical Trust.

The pedigree of the Prichard family, a copy of which was given me by my cousin Mathew Prichard proved invaluable; but I also relied on *A History of* Brecknockshire by Jones and Glanusk, *Welsh Genealogies AD300-1400 (7 vols)* by P. C. Bartrum, University of Wales Press, *The Genealogies of Morgan and Glamorgan* by George T. Clarke, and *The Genealogy of Descendants of Prichards* by The Rev. Thomas Gregory Smart (to rebut assertions contained in *A History of Monmouthshire* by Sir Joseph Bradney). I have made use of *The Complete Peerage; Burke's Irish Family Records* and *Burke's Landed Gentry;* and *The Dictionary of National Biography (DNB)* and the newer *ONDB.* I have quoted from *A History of England* by G. M. Trevelyan; *The Kings Peace* by C. V. Wedgwood; *Marlborough* by Corelli Barnett and *The Black Death* by Philip Ziegler. I have received invaluable advice from Professor Rees Davies, Chichele Professor of Medieval History at All Souls College, Oxford, and Professor J. Beverley Smith, University of Wales, Aberystwyth, both of whom were kind enough to read the original text of this history and suggest revisions and corrections, which have been incorporated into this edition. I completed the original version in July 1999. Since then I have discovered a great deal more about the family. First, my cousin, Massimo Brooke a year or two before his untimely death, let me have the Ingham and Whitaker genealogies and these prompted me to include an account of both families' connection with Sicily and the Marsala wine trade. That led me to a meeting with Raleigh Trevelyan; and I have borrowed heavily from his books *Princes under the Volcano* (since reprinted as a paper back) and *The Companion Guide to Sicily.* Another book covering the subject is *Palaces of Sicily* by Gioacchio Lanza Tomasi and Angheli Zalapi (published in New York by Rizzoli). An article by Irene D. Neu *An*

English Businessman in Sicily 1806-1861 in *The Business History Review,* Vol. XXXI Winter 1957 No. 4 also proved invaluable. Alice Renton's *Tyrant or Victim* and Angeline Goreau's introduction to the Penguin Edition of *Agnes Grey* by Anne Bronte provided information about the latter's employment by the Inghams of Blake Hall. By far the fullest account of the life of Nathaniel Wallich (my great-great-grandfather) is contained in *The European Discovery of the Indian Flora* by Ray Desmond. Royal Botanic Gardens and Oxford University Press, 1992. I have borrowed from it (and the *DNB and ONDB*) very extensively. I have looked at some of Nathaniel Wallich's remarkable collection of specimens in the Herbarium at the Royal Botanic Gardens at Kew. I joined The Welcome Library to examine some of Nathaniel's letters and the remarkable collection of papers of his son, George Charles Wallich. Information about George Charles also came from *The Journal of the Society for the History of Natural History.*

My original brief reference to my great uncle, Horace Wallich, became much longer as a result of the researches of my cousin Vanora Bennett, contained in her vastly entertaining and informative book about modern Russia and caviar, *The Taste of Dreams*, Headline Book Publishing, 2003.

Wild Wales by George Borrow, *Alfred George Edwards, Archbishop of Wales* by George Lerry and material from *Apollo Magazine* were sources for chapters on the Edwards family.

In 2008 Ann and I visited Indonesia to see something of the country where her uncle Guy L'Estrange and so many of her relatives and forebears had worked for the Far East trading company Maclaine Watson & Co. This led me to research its history and to write a paper about the contribution that the McLean and McNeill families made to it. I am grateful to Professor G. Roger Knight of Adelaide University for his invaluable assistance. I have incorporated material from that paper in the main text and included the whole of it as an appendix.

Relations and friends have all helped, but sadly gaps remain which could have been filled if only I had begun my researches while my parents and Ann's were still alive.

Introduction.

A family's development is rather like that of a great river. Some streams, at first hardly discernible, rise in the hills from tiny springs and boggy marshland, perhaps losing themselves briefly, before reappearing again a little stronger and a little easier to identify. Small they may be, but we come across them early as we walk the hills and picnic on their banks. Some grow quickly and vigorously, tumbling over rocky beds and into deep ravines that are the proof of the effect that they have had on the landscape. They are joined along the way by tributaries that add to their volume and their force. They may lose themselves again from time to time in ravines and woods or as their waters pass invisibly through reservoirs and lakes; but each time they reappear our knowledge of them grows and we become more fascinated by the variety of life and activity that they sustain. Other streams may appear later when they are already large and slow moving, emerging from the cover of vast forests and misty marshes. Widely differing in their characteristics and in the state of their development, they join up one by one and come together to form a single great river that flows out to join the ocean, perhaps through a delta formed by the many branches of the main stream.

Families develop in much the same way. We find scraps of evidence way back in the mists of time about some ancestors who are like those little streams on the high hills. We may stumble on others, a few generations later who have in some dramatic way made their impact on history that like river gorges cannot be missed. Others may only appear much later because though their scale and importance is now unmistakeable, their meanderings were previously lost in unmapped forests. The meanders themselves may be significant. Just as two separate streams of different origin may by pure chance come close together, but not meet and join until many miles further on when their characteristics are quite different, so two branches of a family may each be involved in a single event of history many generations before the blood lines mix. In an equally unexpected way the river may rejoin an old bed and a family may find itself living out its life in places on which it had an impact many generations previously. Finally, we see the most recent generations subdivide, and we become interested in the aunts, uncles, brothers, sisters and cousins.

There are great families who have played so important a part in history that there are records that make it possible to recount the story in detail. There are others about which arduous research will produce few facts. This is an account of an ordinary family about which histories have not been written or detailed records kept, but which has left a clear trail behind it. I inherited some incomplete family trees, old papers unsorted in drawers, a few portraits, an 18th century silver coffee pot, and the names and addresses of the many cousins of my wife and myself. Personal interest and the hope that at some time in the future children and grandchildren might be curious about their origins prompted the research that made the telling of this story possible. Before we begin at the beginning I will make only two other observations. The first is that there is a pattern here that must be very typical of a huge number of other families and which arises from the manner in which social structures have developed in this country. The second is that the intermingling of English, Welsh, Scottish and Irish blood (and the history of those nations) that has produced my children and grandchildren is a characteristic of families that is also unlikely to be exceptional. That fact appears to me to be significant when confronted by the current wave of nationalist sentiment and at a time when the unity of the United Kingdom is under threat. Throughout my political life I have proclaimed my pride in being Welsh, but my equal pride in being British. My grandchildren have every reason to take pride in their common heritage from all four nations in the British Isles.

Chapter 1.   The Beginning.

The beginning was far away and in the remotest parts of those high hills. Indeed, I suppose that if modern science is right the very beginning was somewhere in Africa! Bold genealogists claim that my Prichard forebears can trace their named descent back to Caradoc Vraich Vras who is said to have been Earl of Hereford and Prince between Wye and Severn between AD 520 and AD570; but three years reading history at Cambridge at least taught me to be sceptical of facts that cannot be substantiated by evidence. The Dark Ages in Wales was an age of bards and the history of the people was passed by word of mouth from generation to generation; but there is a notable lack of written documentation. Certainly, it would be both a foolish and a rash man who recited with confidence the names of the sixteen generations of Welsh princes that are said to have come between Caradoc Vraich Vras and the Norman Conquest, although that does not prevent them being solemnly set out in the family tree.

It is about the time of the Conquest, or a little before, that the mists begin to clear a little and several strong little streams appear.

Two of them were in Wales and the third, rising in Brittany, flowed first through Norfolk but later washed the Marches of Wales with furious and destructive force. My father's mother was a Prichard; and he was born at Pwllywrach, near Cowbridge in Glamorgan, which had become the family home when his grandfather had married a Thomas in 1858. The claim of the Prichards to descend directly from Maenarch ap Dryffryn, Prince of Brecon in the early 11th century can be made with a much higher degree of historical probability than that to Caradoc Vraich Vras. We know a good deal about Maenarch's eldest son who was slain by Bernard Neufmarché in a battle near the river Usk in 1090. The Prichards descend from a younger brother, Rhys Goch, Lord of Ystrad Yw and from the five succeeding Lords of Ystrad Yw who carried the descent down to the mid 13th century. It is with the arrival of Rhys Goch that history provides the first odd quirk of fate. Ystrad Yw (the vale of the yew trees) was the name given at that time to the district around what is now Crickhowell. In the early part of the 10th century it formed part of one of the seven cantrefs of the lordship of Glamorgan. The parish of Llanbedr, a little to the east of the town, is still properly styled Llanbedr Ystrad Yw. When I took the title Lord Crickhowell in 1987 I had no idea that nine hundred years earlier Welsh ancestors had held the Lordship and had continued to hold some level of responsibility after the Normans introduced their own Lords around the first motte at Tretower, built by Picard, a vassal of Bernard Neufmarché (the lord of Brecon), a short distance down the valley from the Welsh settlement. The separation of the English and Welsh administrations was common in Wales until late in the Middle Ages, even when the communities were in close proximity. The Welsh and English were also treated separately at law and their affairs were often dealt with in separate courts. It is likely that the Norman and English settlers were grouped close to the castle and the village, with the Welsh primarily in the uplands. This was the situation around Hay; and no doubt things were not very different at the southern end of the Black Mountains.

The coincidence of history is even more remarkable than the link of titles. On the font of the Church of Patricio (of which I am the Rector's warden and where my father, mother and eldest brother are buried) is the inscription Menhir me fecit in tempor [ie tempore] Genillin. Menhir made me in the time of Genillin. The historians tell us that Genillin was Cynyllin Voel ap Rhys, the son of Rhys Goch, and that he is known to have been alive in 1056. It is on this evidence that we can have a good deal of confidence about the existence of a pre-Norman church at Patricio. The Book of Llandaff (Liber Landavensis), in the main compiled in the 1120s, records that Herewald, Bishop of Llandaff, 1056-1103 consecrated the church of Llanfihangel Cwmdu and the churches of Llanbedr and Merthyr Issue (Patricio) and committed them to the care of Matgwith. In the struggle over territory between two forceful later Bishops in the 12th century, Bernard of St Davids and Urban of Llandaff, Bernard emerged largely triumphant; and one result was to be the transfer of both Ystrad Yw and the neighbouring Ewyas into the diocese of St Davids; but that is to step too far ahead. For the time being we can leave the Prichards until the stream turns south and provides fresh interest in the 13th century.

Another Welsh tributary can be traced to its source in Glamorgan. The Thomas family is one of many in Glamorgan that claim descent from Jestyn ap Gwrgan, chief lord of Glamorgan at the time of the conquest, who was overcome by Sir Robert Fitz-Hamon in 1089 and died in 1090. Such are the complexities of Glamorgan genealogies, with much intermarriage among the families, that I will do no more than acknowledge the claim at this stage; but I will return to this particular rivulet when it grows stronger and merges with a branch of the Herberts in the 15th century.

This is the moment to move to Norfolk and our first glimpse of a particularly strong and turbulent river that was to have a momentous impact on the history of Wales; was to have powerful effects in Ireland; and the genes of which are clearly discernible in the family to this day. My wife's mother was a L'Estrange. The first member of the family recorded in England was Rhiwallon Extraneus, sometimes called Roland L'Estrange who appears in two deeds during the reign of Henry I (1100-1135). He originally came from Brittany and appears to have been a close friend of Alan fitz Flaald and other companions of King Henry in his youth. Henry had been Lord of the Cotentin (known to us as the Cherbourg peninsular). The fitz Flaald family from Dol in Brittany became anglicised as Fitz Alan, and the relationship with Roland continued both in Norfolk and the Welsh Marches. Roland married Matilda Le Brun, the daughter and heiress of Ralf Le Brun (otherwise known as Ralph de Hunstanton) who was mesne lord of Hunstanton at the time of the Domesday survey as a vassal of Roger Bigod, Earl of Norfolk; and who held a considerable estate covering nine or ten parishes bordering the Wash during this period. In addition to the land that Ralph inherited from his father or that he acquired himself, he inherited land near Thetford in Suffolk from his wife Helewisa. Some of the land at Hunstanton that came to the L'Estranges after Ralph's death remained in the ownership of the family until the present day.

For the purpose of this history what is much more important is that by early in the reign of Henry II three of Roland's sons, John (usually identified as John I), Hamon and Guy, were enfeoffed of land in Shropshire on the borders of Wales. The new men whom Henry I had brought over from France were now to be used by his grandson, Henry II, as feudal tenants on the Welsh Marches. There, the crown had a particular need for capable subjects owing loyalty to the king, rather than powerful barons with their own interests to pursue. This was the age in which the recurring theme was tension and conflict between the crown, anxious to increase the power of central government, and the baronage determined to resist, particularly in the Marches where its independent power was greatest. It was Guy (Eudo), the third son of Roland who initially played the major role. He was appointed Sheriff of Shropshire on the death of William fitz Alan; he was also appointed custos or warden of Oswestry, the most advanced post on the north-west frontier of the Welsh March and was keeper of the two royal castles of Bridgenorth and Shrewsbury.

Chapter 2.   The Welsh Wars.

We know that Guy played some part in the attempts of Henry II to subdue the unruly Welsh, and in 1164 he held hostages that the king brought back from his disastrous third expedition into Wales. Guy stood by the king during the feudal revolt of 1173-4 and was present at the Council of Northampton in 1177, in which the foundations of the judicial structure of England were laid. He died in 1179, a little more than a year after his elder brother John, and he left no sons.

The family had been granted property at Knockin in Shropshire very early in the reign of Henry II, and John (II) now succeeded to the property and was probably the first to build a castle there. However, it was not long before he had much wider responsibilities than the protection of his own property. During the reign of Richard I, a king who was almost always abroad, John had the custody of Pole Castle (now Powis Castle) on behalf of the crown. On King John's succession in 1199 John L'Estrange became one of the kings most trusted servants. This was the time when Llywelyn ap Iorwerth (the Great), Prince of Gwynedd, taking advantage of the weakness of the English king, was extending his power to cover the whole of Wales except for the Marcher Lordships in the south. There is a contemporary document that states that John L'Estrange did much damage to the people of the Welsh Prince. In retaliation Llywelyn destroyed the castle that John had built at Ruyton and imprisoned some of his men. In an ensuing fight John L'Estrange was struck in the face by a lance and bore the mark of his wound for the rest of his life. In 1204 the King used John L'Estrange, together with the Bishops of Bangor and St Asaph, William fitz Alan, and others, to send a safe conduct to Llywelyn.

John must have been something of a diplomat. Loyal to a bad king and frequently entrusted by him with important tasks, and appointed by that king Sheriff of Stafford and Shropshire in the final disastrous year of a notorious reign, John L'Estrange was, none-the-less, soon in favour with those around the young King Henry III. He was one of those present at the council held in Bristol on November 11, 1216 to meet the new King and his guardians. Llywelyn the Great, after his triumphant march through Wales, thought it wise to come to terms with the new king; and John L'Estrange was once again one of those entrusted with safe conducts, this time to those Welshmen sent by Llywelyn to Worcester to do homage. In 1223 he was one of those appointed by the King to confer with Llywelyn and to report in writing about land that the Prince had seized from Marcher lords. In 1232 John was probably appointed constable of Montgomery Castle when the King quarrelled with Hubert de Burgh. At any rate it was in his custody in 1233 when he was sent a mandate to release it and the castle of Sneth to William de Boeles. John died at the end of 1233 or early in 1234 at the age of about eighty, having for sixty years been the servant successively of Henry II, Richard Coeur-de-Lion, John and Henry III.

While John (II) was still alive, his son, John (III), crossed to France in 1230 with the young Henry III and his army in an attempt to regain the English possessions that had been lost by King John, and was with the King in Brittany, Anjou, Poitou, and Gascony. Four years later he succeeded his father in possession of the L'Estrange fiefs. His occupation of them lasted from 1234 to 1269. It was during that time that the power, first of Llywelyn the Great, and then of Llywelyn ap Gruffudd (the Last) reached its peak. Just as John was taking up his family responsibilities King Henry found himself in serious conflict with his nobles, and for a brief time Richard, Earl of Pembroke, the Earl Marshal and other nobles entered into a league with Llywelyn (and their forces completely destroyed the original stone castle at Abergavenny). In 1234 a truce was made, and John was one of those who swore on the king's behalf that the truce would be observed. A mandate was issued to John and three other commissioners to conduct Llywelyn's son, Dafydd, to pay homage to the King. By 1235 John was constable of Montgomery; and in the following year we again find him swearing a truce with Llywelyn on behalf of the King. In the years that followed John is repeatedly found acting on behalf of the King in attempts to deal with infringements of the truce; and on more than one occasion is given responsibility for providing safe conduct for Welsh envoys. In 1240 he was appointed by patent to the custody of the county and castle of Chester; and in practice he held the high office of *Justice of Chester*, the earldom of the palatine county being in the King's hands. In the same year he was doing building works on behalf of the King at Shrewsbury, and he also hurried off with three others to Cardigan to settle a land dispute. In the following year a patent gives notification that John, to whom the King had committed the castles of Montgomery, Shrewsbury, Bridgenorth, and Chester, had sworn on the Holy Gospels before the King, and bound himself by Letters Patent, that 'in the event of the King's death he would deliver the said castles to Eleanor, his Queen, to the use of Edward, his son and heir, or of another heir begotten by the said King of the said Queen'. Edward was at that date an infant under two years of age.

In 1241 John L'Estrange was placed in supreme command of the Marches in the face of the threatening posture of Dafydd, son of Llywelyn ap Iorwerth, who had died on 11 April 1240. Henry III soon showed that he would not allow the son to enjoy the status of his father. The two met at Gloucester six weeks after Llywelyn's death; and although Dafydd was confirmed in possession of the territories which his father had held *de jure*, Henry insisted that the allegiance of the lesser Welsh rulers belonged exclusively to the English crown. Later that year Henry compelled Dafydd to hand over his elder brother, Gruffudd, who was then imprisoned in London's White Tower, from which he fell to his death on St David's Day, 1244, while attempting to escape. With the possible competition of his brother thus removed, Dafydd attempted to recreate some of the old alliances; and he sought the support of the Papacy for his claims. Henry retaliated with a campaign of remarkable ferocity in Gwynedd; the Pope rejected Dafydd's supplication to be a direct vassal of the Papacy; and in 1246 Dafydd died.

It was against this background that John L'Estrange had been given the responsibility of safeguarding the Marches against any Welsh attack. 'A mandate was issued to all the barons, knight's &c., in the counties of Chester, Salop, and Stafford, to come in force when summoned by le Strange to defend the King's lieges of Wales against attack'. John was also keeper of Clun and Oswestry; and was given responsibilities extending into Clwyd. He was virtually military governor of the whole of the North March. As part of his preparations John began building what became the castle of Diserth near Rhuddlan, which became the chief border castle in this region until Edward I built the new Rhuddlan after 1277. He was given the task of retaining for the King the district of Mold and of restoring to certain barons land that had been taken from them by Llywelyn. By his activities, he laid a solid foundation for the King's power between the Conwy and the Clwyd. The king conceded lordship over these newly conquered lands in North Wales to his son, Edward, in 1254.

John also made possible the restitution of Gruffudd ap Gwenwynwyn to his dominions in mid Wales. It was surely no coincidence that, later, John's daughter, Hawyse, would marry Gruffudd, whose lands lay adjacent to his own castle at Knockin. The responsibilities John held were no sinecure. The records reveal that he was frequently required to raise troops and money, to cut down woods to make the passage of the royal armies easier, and from time to time to fight. Diserth Castle was besieged by Dafydd in 1245 and John may well have been inside it. His job was not made easier by the king's conduct of affairs. J. Beverley Smith, in his life of Llywelyn, records that in the same year, 1245, "delay in launching his offensive cost him dearly. John Lestrange's appeal for aid became more vociferous, remonstrating with the king that £10,000 would no longer be enough to accomplish what earlier might have been done for £1,000. Even so, moving ahead of the main forces summoned to Chester, Lestrange secured Tegeingl and Henry was then able to advance through Rhos to Degannwy while forces from Ireland took Anglesey". The chronicler Matthew Paris wrote that after the Treaty of Woodstock (1247) "Wales has been pulled down to nothing".

Not long after these events John ceased to hold the onerous office of Justice of Chester; and in 1248 he was relieved of some of his responsibilities for the defence of the Welsh March, and he handed over a number of the castles for which he had been responsible. He was then about 55 years old. However, in his later years he continued from time to time to serve the King.

J. Beverley Smith describes how John was sent to Gwynedd in 1256 when it dawned on the king's council that Llywelyn was on the point of invading. The historian comments that though we have no means of knowing what the envoy was empowered to negotiate, it would be likely that he was sent to discuss matters of importance which the king had neglected to consider until the eleventh hour. "No one would have greater cause to wonder at the king's ineptitude than Lestrange himself, who could recall Henry's failure to respond to successive requests for the resources to meet an earlier Welsh challenge, and would remember the harsh treatment meted out to the very men who had urged prudent action in good time".

The story now moves on to the remarkable children of John who all made a singular contribution to English and Welsh history, and made a mark as well in the Crusader kingdoms. In the middle years of his reign, Henry III was opposed by many of his barons under the leadership of Simon de Montfort. The growing hostility of the barons to the king, and particularly of the Marcher lords who resented the extension of the Royal authority, is well illustrated by the reaction of Walter de Clifford, lord of Llandovery, who was so incensed when he received a summons from Henry III that he forced the messenger to eat it, seal and all. The King was, in effect, deposed when the government of the country passed into the hands of a baronial council, led by de Montfort, which ruled in the King's name. Disorder in England meant opportunity for the Welsh. Dafydd had been succeeded by his nephews, Llywelyn ap Gruffudd and his elder brother Owain. While it was not the weakness of the English King that then provoked the Welsh rebellion, by the time its initial success was secured the baronial revolt prevented effective counter measures. In the years 1255-1256 Llywelyn made himself sole ruler of Gwynedd and during the following two years swept through Wales. Gruffudd ap Gwenwynwyn was again driven out of most of his possessions, although with the aid of John L'Estrange and the royal forces he was able to retain possession of the castle of Welshpool and some of the adjacent lands. In 1258 representatives of the ruling houses of Powys, Deheubarth, and Glamorgan acknowledged Llywelyn, not only as their leader but as their lord.

For the next four years Llywelyn refrained from further campaigns and tried during a series of truces to win the King's recognition of his position and title, despite damaging incursions into Wales by major figures such as Roger Mortimer and John L'Estrange, who carried the war into parts of Powis. In 1262 Llywelyn advanced again, this time into the lordships of Brecon and Abergavenny, and Peter de Montfort (to be distinguished from Simon), who had been sent to take custody of the lordship of Abergavenny reported an attack on Llanfihangel Crucornau. (just two miles from where we now live in Wales). This attack posed a threat to The Three Castles of Gwent, that is the lordships of Grosmont, Skenfrith and White Castle. De Montfort's message made clear that this threat was not just posed by an army operating in alien territory, but that "all the men of the Welsh nation in the lordships of Brecon, Talgarth and Blaenllyfni, Elfael, Ystrad Yu, Tal-y-bont and Crughywel had turned to Llywelyn". One wonders whether at this moment my Prichard forbears, descendants of Rhys Goch of Ystrad Yu, were engaged in battle on the Welsh side while Ann's L'Estrange ancestors were fighting for the King. Peter de Montfort feared that the men of Abergavenny would join Llywelyn. It was a major crisis; but the Welsh Prince's army was defeated in a crucial battle at the foot of the Blorenge mountain, just to the west of the town.

Although deserted by his brother, Dafydd, sometime in the summer of 1263 Llywelyn allied himself to Simon de Montfort at about the moment that he was pressing hard on Montgomery where John L'Estrange had custody of the royal lordship. John suffered a defeat. After taking a strong force into Welsh territory, his soldiers suffered heavy losses as the Welsh fell upon them when "laden with spoil" they made their return. Simon de Montfort was victorious over the royal forces at Lewes in May 1264; and in June, at Pipton near Glasbury, he recognised Llywelyn as Prince of Wales and overlord of the *magnates Wallie*. For Simon de Montfort it was to be a short lived triumph, because two months later on 1 August 1265 he was defeated and killed at Evesham.

Llywelyn's successes were to continue for a few more years. In 1267, through the intervention of the Papal Legate, he obtained the recognition that he wanted from Henry III in the Treaty of Montgomery; but he had been making powerful enemies, some within his own family. He had denied Owain, his elder brother his rights as the first born, and his younger brothers Dafydd and Rhodri also had rights to a share in their patrimony. Even more serious was the enmity of the Marcher lords, such as Gilbert de Clare, with his great castle at Caerffili which Llywelyn attacked in 1271. From 1272 onwards de Clare, who had successfully secured northern Glamorgan, and two other barons, Bohun, and Mortimer, became increasingly formidable foes. In 1274 there was a dramatic addition to the ranks of the Prince's enemies when his brother, Dafydd, and his chief vassal, Gruffudd ap Gwenwynwyn, fled to England, leaving behind evidence of a plot to kill him in which the L'Estrange family may well have been involved.

In England the royal power passed to Henry's son, the Lord Edward, victorious at Evesham, who ascended the throne in 1272. To a king such as Edward I the chaos in the Marches was intolerable. For him the final provocation was Llywelyn's announcement that he intended to marry Elinor, the daughter of Simon de Montfort. Llywelyn was prevented from doing so when she was captured by the English as she crossed the channel on her way to Wales. In 1276 Edward declared Llywelyn a rebel and prepared for war.

CHAPTER 3. EDWARD I AND THE CONQUEST OF WALES.

This, then, was the stage on which the children of John L'Estrange (III) played their parts. If we were to stay in the main river of genealogical descent we would concern ourselves only with John (IV) and hurry on quite quickly to John (V), first Lord Strange of Knockin; but the siblings are far too interesting for us to do that. John (IV) died accidentally in the Severn in the autumn of 1275. During the baronial wars of the previous reign he seems to have espoused the cause of the barons, unlike his younger brother Hamon who remained loyal throughout. When those wars began he was bailiff of Montgomery Castle; and a Welsh chronicle tells us that in 1263 he made a night attack on Ceri and Cydewain, but was surprised by the Welsh, who assembled in great force and slew 200 of his men, forcing him to retreat. In revenge he burnt the barn of Abermule. More significant from the point of view of the family history, he made a brilliant marriage. His wife was Joan, daughter of Roger de Somery, of Dudley Castle, Staffordshire, by his first wife Nicola, sister and co-heir of Hugh de Albini, last Earl of Arundel of that line. The marriage eventually added greatly to the territorial influence of the family. The marriage of his sister Hawyse to Gruffudd ap Gwenwynwyn had taken place in 1242; she must have had a remarkable life in the company of a Welshman whose fortunes and loyalties swung back and forward like a pendulum during these years.

John's younger brother, Hamon, had been an intimate companion of Edward in his youth; and both had accompanied Henry III on his expedition to Bordeaux in 1253. He was one of the close friends whom Edward gathered around him to form the nucleus of the party which later led him to victory and thus to the throne, but during the baronial conflicts of the previous reign he had held the castles of Montgomery, Bridgenorth and Shrewsbury on behalf of the barons and had been one of those in the first outbreak of violence when the baronial wars broke out in 1263. Although Henry III was to live for another ten years, it was in that period of conflict that Edward took the lead as the champion of royal power and began skilfully to win over to the royal cause the very marcher lords who had triggered it, Hamon and his brother Roger among them, and they were present with the royal forces at Lewes.

Both escaped capture at that royal defeat. A contemporary chronicle relates how Hamon, following the battle, returned to Wales and ravaged the Welsh Marches with such cruelty that the natives sought refuge in the churches.

Another contemporary account describes how Hamon and other knights who had escaped from Lewes attempted to rescue Edward from his captivity at Wallingford in Berkshire. According to this chronicle, Edward himself appealed to them to desist in the face of the threat by the defenders to attach Edward to a mangonel (a military engine for hurling stones) and to catapult him into the ranks of his would be rescuers. Edward was soon to escape, and in the following year (1265) he defeated de Montford at the Battle of Evesham. There are good grounds for thinking that Hamon was present at the battle.

In the meantime, despite his L'Estrange upbringing and his marriage to Hawyse, Gruffudd ap Gwenwynwyn had entered into an alliance with Llywelyn. The switch seems to have been prompted by a struggle over land on the Welsh border and perhaps by the involvement of Hamon and his associates in the confused events that marked the outbreak of the civil war.

In the same year as the battle of Evesham Llywelyn captured and destroyed the castle of Hawarden on the border between Wales and Cheshire. A royal army was sent against him under the command of Hamon L'Estrange and Maurice fitz Gerald. Llywelyn put these two English knights to flight and many of their troops were killed. Two years later peace was concluded on Llywelyn's terms by the Treaty of Montgomery, and Hamon was among those present at the ford on the river Severn below the castle at Montgomery where Llywelyn did homage and swore fealty.

At this point in the story of the remarkable L'Estranges we find ourselves joining the crusades. With a degree of pacification in both England and Wales, Prince Edward, encouraged by his father, Henry III, set out on a crusade in the summer of 1270. He was in his early thirties. With him was his wife, Eleanor of Castile, and about one thousand men, among them Hamon and his younger brother, Roger. Edward's intention had been to join King Louis of France at Tunis and sail on with him to the Holy Land, but he arrived in Africa to find the King dead and the French troops about to return home. He wintered in Sicily and sailed on next spring to Cyprus and then to Acre, where he landed on 9 May 1271. Steven Runciman tells us that Edward was horrified by the state of affairs he found in the Christian territory known as Outremer. His diplomatic initiatives came to nothing; he contented himself with a few minor raids across the frontier, and by the spring of 1272 he realised that he was wasting his time. All that he could do was to arrange a truce that would preserve Outremer for the time being. On 22 May 1272, a peace was signed between the Sultan and the Government of Acre; but on

16 June 1272, an assassin, disguised as a native Christian, penetrated the Prince's chamber and stabbed him with a poisoned dagger. The wound was not fatal, but Edward was seriously ill for some months. Finally, he embarked from Acre on 22 September 1272, and returned to England to find himself King. Robert L'Estrange returned with him; but Hamon, known ever-after as the Crusader, remained. In that same year 1272 Hamon married Isabella, the eldest daughter John II of Ibelin. She was Dowager Queen of Cyprus and, following the death of her father, was to become holder of the lordship of Beirut, which had been the chief mainland fief of King Hugh of Cyprus. She had been left a virgin widow in 1267, but her virginity was of short duration. Her notorious lack of chastity and, in particular, her liaison with Julian of Sidon, provoked a Papal Bull, which strongly urged her to remarry. In 1272 she gave herself and her lordship to Hamon L'Estrange. He distrusted King Hugh, and on his deathbed next year he put his wife and her fief under the protection of the Sultan Baibars. Poor Hamon had not enjoyed the company of his wife for very long. When, after his death, Hugh tried to carry off the widow to Cyprus in order to remarry her to a candidate of his choice, the sultan at once cited the pact that Hamon had made and demanded her return. The High Court gave the King no support. He was obliged to send Isabella back to Beirut, where a mameluke guard was installed to protect her. Isabella married two more husbands before her death in about 1282, when Beirut passed to her sister Eschiva, the wife of Humphrey of Montfort, who was a loyal friend of the King. Hugh then resumed control of the fief.

At this point we must introduce Roger L'Estrange, for he played a part in the war which Edward waged against Llywelyn in 1277, and a dominant part in the war of 1282 and the events which followed it. Roger, the brother of John L'Estrange (IV), Hamon and Hawyse, is referred to by contemporaries as 'of Ellesmere', his principal feudal territory, which lies on the border between Shropshire and Wales. He had fought with the royal forces against de Montfort at Lewes and had made good his escape when the royal army suffered defeat. After the royal victory at Evesham he became Sheriff of Yorkshire and custodian of the castle of York and at the same time custodian of the Castle of the Peak in Derbyshire.

In 1277 Edward invaded Wales. One of his armies, under Roger L'Estrange and Roger Mortimer entered southern Powys. Work was started on building a new royal castle at Builth. Another army, based on Carmarthen and Llandovery, penetrated into Cardiganshire where a start was made on the building of the castle at Llandabarn (Aberystwyth). Meanwhile the main army under the King approached Snowdonia along the coast of North Wales from Chester. The King requisitioned ships from the Cinque Ports which landed troops on Anglesey. The occupation of Anglesey deprived Llywelyn of the corn harvest and in the face of this disaster he had no alternative but to capitulate. The Treaty of Aberconway confined him to Gwynedd. He retained the by now hollow title of Prince of Wales. His treacherous brother, David, who had fought on the side of the King, was installed in Denbighshire, and Roger L'Estrange's brother-in-law and sister, Gruffudd ap Gwenwynwen and Hawyse, were restored to southern Powys. In 1278 Roger was appointed to the custody of the castle of Dinas Bran overlooking the Dee at Llangollen. The ruins of the later castle of Dinas Bran, built by L'Estrange's successor, still look down upon the town of Llangollen.

Five uneasy years followed the war of 1277. The King released Eleanor de Montford and allowed her marriage with Llywelyn, and indeed Edward was present when the ceremony took place in Worcester cathedral. The castle of Builth, by then in royal hands, was rebuilt as a massive fortress. During these years Roger L'Estrange was employed by the king on a duty very different from that of pacifying the Welsh. This time the King was concerned with the claims of the church. When the Archbishop of Canterbury summoned a convocation of bishops in 1280 the king, suspecting trouble, sent Roger and Hugh fitz Otto, the steward of the royal household, with orders to instruct the prelates to agree nothing that might diminish the rights and interests of the crown.

Then tension rose again in Wales; and when in 1282 the first blow was struck by Dafydd, the king's former ally, the conflagration spread rapidly. The scene was the same castle of Hawarden where Hamon had received a bloody nose in the hands of Llywelyn seventeen years before. After Dafydd had attacked and captured it, Llywelyn moved south and plundered the land of the king's allies in the vale of Tywi. Edward ordered a massive retaliation. The strategy was the same as that which had proved so successful in 1277. The king requisitioned the ships of the Cinque Ports and assembled them off the north Wales coast. He advanced his northern army from Chester, first to Rhuddlan, and then to the river Conwy. The central army, based on Montgomery, was commanded at first by Roger Mortimer, and the southern army, based on Carmarthen, by William de Valance, Earl of Pembroke. Roger L'Estrange was given custody of the new castle at Builth. His garrison there consisted of nine troopers and forty foot, shortly afterwards re-enforced by two knights and six further troopers. When Roger Mortimer died in October 1282 Roger l'Estrange was appointed commander of the central army, the custody of Builth castle passing to John Giffard. Since L'Estrange could not claim the prestige of a Mortimer as a leading Marcher lord, his appointment indicates the trust placed in him by the King. Not only was he widely experienced in the service of the King, but he had the further advantage that his brother-in-law, Gruffudd ap Gwenwynwyn, was a supporter of the Crown and the most powerful Welsh lord in central Wales.

In the spring of 1283 the southern army advanced to lay siege to Castell y Bere where it was joined by a force brought from the marches by Roger L'Estrange. There were about 2000 men drawn from L'Estrange's own lordship of Ellesmere and from Knockin and other lordships on the march. His men were on de Valance's account roll. The army met with initial success and in June it took Carreg Cennen. The victory was short lived. While they were returning, laden with booty, the short distance to their castle of Dynevor in the Tywy valley they were overwhelmed by the Welsh and heavily defeated. In September the King took Ruthin and in the following month Denbigh fell. By the autumn the royal forces were on the east bank of the Conwy and Anglesey was occupied by troops landed from the ships from the Cinque Ports. These events drew Llywelyn back to join his brother, Dafydd, in defence of the mountain fortress of Snowdonia. Edward planned to assault Snowdonia from two directions. He had his army on the Conwy and ordered that a bridge of boats should be constructed from Anglesey to the mainland so that his troops on the island under the command of Luke de Tany, a former Constable of Gascony, could launch an attack on the flank. On the 6th November, without orders from the King, de Tany with a body of horse and foot crossed the bridge of boats only to be attacked by a strong Welsh force. In the struggle that followed the bridge of boats collapsed and de Tany and many of his knights were drowned. In the face of this disaster Edward, still at Rhuddlan, issued orders for a new and vital phase in the conflict.

Llywelyn then took the opportunity to lead an army to mid Wales where the death of Roger Mortimer the previous month seemed to create an opportunity. A powerful tradition in Wales is that he was lured there by false promises of support and that Mortimer's sons, Edmund and Roger, were involved in the plot. In a message to the King (the original written in Norman French) sent in the first week of December,1282, Roger L'Estrange first reported that the enemy were 'beyond Berwyn and beyond Merugge, which mountains are so boggy and inhospitable that no army can enter them without putting your men in great danger'; but then at the end added 'the night this letter was written news reached me that Llywelyn had descended into the land of the Lord Gruffudd and therefore I am going there'.

J. Beverley Smith, the most recent biographer of Llywelyn, gives us a detailed account of Roger's role at this critical moment. "After the death of the elder Mortimer the direction of the king's operations in the march were entrusted to Roger Lestrange, and, whatever may have been the information or the instinct which brought him to do so, he had gathered a mighty force in the vicinity of Builth by the time the prince arrived there. In two letters written to Edward, Lestrange reveals a detailed knowledge of the wherabouts of Llywelyn's forces and of the prince himself.......This may be no more than good evidence of the competence of a field commander, but Lestrange had something of the inner knowledge of the Welsh nation, witness his ability to seek out some of Llywelyn's possessions after his death. Certainly, there can be no doubt of the key role that he played in the death of the prince. Lestrange had good reason to look to Edward for some reward after the conquest-- Penllyn and Edeirnion or Maelor Saesneg he thought--and the king's failure to provide for him from the spoils of war is astonishing. The key co-ordinator of military activity in the march after the failure of the archbishop's negotiations, Lestrange may have benefited a good deal from his access to knowledge of what was happening on the Welsh side. Additionally, as suggested already, decisions taken by Llywelyn and his confidants may have been influenced by what was fed to them, with or without the king's knowledge, by those magnates of the march who had useful associations with laymen and churchmen in close attendance on the prince.......Undoubtedly the person mainly responsible for the deployment of the forces which confronted Llywelyn before Builth, one with close links with the soldiers most involved in the action in which the prince was killed, and the person who sent the king the crucial communiqué from the battlefield, Roger Lestrange may have brought to his task more than the qualities of an astute military commander. His role in the prince's death was well known in the immediate aftermath of the event. It is to him, even perhaps more than Edmund Mortimer, that we need to look most closely in any estimate of the influence which might have brought Llywelyn to meet his death in the march of Wales...........

Llywelyn appears to have led a large army to the lordship of Builth. And, whatever brought them to the area--good intelligence on the part of the king's commanders or something much more intriguing-- there to meet him were substantial forces........The military might of the whole march from Oswestry to Hereford gathered together at the place where Llywelyn was to fall."

The stage was set for what for the Welsh was to be an historic tragedy. Having reached the neighbourhood of Builth on the 11th December, Llywelyn occupied the high ground of Llanganten just north of the Irfon, a river flowing east which joins the Wye at Builth. Roger L'Estrange, who could rely on the castle of Builth as his base, moved his forces along the south bank of the Irfon until later in the day the two armies were facing each other. According to the chronicler, Walter of Gisborough, between them the river was crossed by a bridge, known as Orewin Bridge which probably stood above the rapids near the village of Cilmeri (Beverley Smith doubts that it existed). It was in the hands of the Welsh and the river was in flood; but a local man told L'Estrange of a ford further upstream where his troops could cross. As dusk was falling a detachment, having crossed the ford, fell upon the flank of the Welsh defenders of the bridge. With the bridge captured L'Estrange's men poured across it. Archers placed among his heavy cavalry caused havoc among the Welsh; Powick states that this is the first example in these wars of the use of archers in open fighting. When the cavalry rode down the Welsh on the higher ground, Llywelyn's forces, armed only with spears, broke and fled.

While these events were unfolding, Llywelyn was not with the main body of his troops. It has been suggested that he may have been seeking to make contact with those forces on the royal side who had promised him support, as Henry of Richmond was to do two hundred years later at Bosworth. Whatever the reason, one Stephen Frankton, a tenant of L'Estrange's at Ellesmere, came upon the Prince with a small group of horsemen and, in a brief skirmish, drove his lance through him. Llywelyn, dying, asked for a priest, but no priest came. Frankton, unaware of the identity of the horseman who he had slain, rode off. When the Prince was recognised, his head was cut off and sent to the King at Rhuddlan, after which it was displayed on the Tower of London. Maud the wife of John Giffard, who held the castle of Builth, was the grand-daughter of Llywelyn the Great, and her intercession with Archbishop Pecham may have been the cause of Llywelyn's body being taken to Abbey Cwm Hir for burial.

After the historic skirmish, Roger sent his second message to the King; 'Know, sire, that the good men whom you placed under my command fought with Llywelyn ap Gruffudd in the land of Builth on Friday next after the feast of St. Nicholas and that Gruffudd is dead, his army broken and the flower of his men killed, as the bearer of this letter will tell you, and believe what he tells you as coming from me'.

Some historians, relying on a contemporary chronicle, have conclude that John Giffard was in command at Orewin Bridge; but Roger's second message leaves no room for doubt that the troops involved were those under his command; and most modern historians confirm that judgement. A letter in Latin, now in the Bibliotheque Nationale in Paris, provides powerful supporting evidence. It was written by Stephen of St George, a royal clerk who later, in 1283, became Edward I's proctor at the papal court. It is the most nearly contemporaneous document, other than Roger's letters, relating to Llywelyn's death. The letter states that the news of Llywelyn's death reached Rome on the 22nd January only about five weeks after it had first reached the King at Rhuddlan. The letter, which refers to the Welsh prince in terms of extraordinary virulence concludes with the words: 'It would be a wonderful thing, and certainly a just one, if, as is commonly reported, a knight estranged by name yet close in loyalty should have exacted the extreme penalty from the rebel and traitor Llywelyn who by the error of his infidelity is estranged indeed'. That play on words suggests that it may have been L'Estrange who struck off the head of the dead Prince, but other evidence indicates that that was not so.

The chronicle of Walter of Gisborough, probably written in the next reign, after reporting that Stephen de Frankton had failed to recognise Llywelyn continues 'Then, as our men were returning after the battle, Stephen went to see who the two men were whom he had wounded, and, when the face of Llywelyn had been seen and recognised, they cut off his head'. Despite the fact that de Frankton is usually accepted as the man who struck the first fatal blow, Smith produces an alternative version based on a different chronicle that it was in fact Sir Robert Body who was responsible, but he, too, was closely associated with Roger L'Estrange. We cannot be certain whether it was Stephen de Frankton or Robert Body; but it does not much matter. The historic fact is that on that day Llywelyn ap Gruffudd was killed and his death brought to an end the Welsh age of the Princes. The sense of Welsh loss was profound and long lasting:

> "When that head fell, men welcomed terror,
> When that head fell, it were better to stop.--
> Why, O my God does the sea not cover the land?
> Why are we left to linger?" *Anon*

Roger L'Estrange played a central role in the subsequent pacification and the capture of Llywelyn's brother Dafydd, who was not mourned. In the first war he had conspired and fought against his brother and in the second, after he had received some reward from the King, he fought with his brother against Edward. Roger L'Estrange evidently exercised some responsibility for the area of what is now Meirionydd after the cessation of hostilities, and probably during this period he made an approach to the crown for the grant of an estate as a reward for his labours. That was not granted, but, in recognition for his services, he was appointed to the onerous, but important, position of Justice of the Forest south of the Trent, with jurisdiction over the whole of southern England. Before then he still had work to do. In 1287 he was involved in putting down another Welsh rising. In1291 he was sent with others as an envoy to Rome to persuade the Pope to withdraw his claim to be the feudal superior of Edward's Scottish kingdom. In 1294 there was yet another Welsh uprising, and once again Roger was involved in raising a force in the central march. In 1295 he was summoned to parliament and thereafter was regularly summoned as a baron. With his nephews, John of Knockin and Fulk of Blackmere, he was one of those who sealed the document sent to the Pope in 1301 which asserted the supremacy of the crown of England over Scotland. The seals from the document of those three L'Estrange barons survive.

Roger L'Estrange left no legitimate heirs. His nephew John (V) accompanied Edward in the Scottish wars; and by reason of a summons to Parliament became the first Lord Strange of Knockin. He was active, but played a less prominent part, in the Welsh wars than did his uncle. After the first Welsh war he received a warm letter of thanks from the King for services over and above those due from him by his feudal tenure, services that put him quite substantially into debt. He played a subordinate role to Roger in the second Welsh war, and again the cost of those services put him into debt, and he was often reduced to the necessity of borrowing money. He served in Gascony in the expedition of 1296 under the King's brother, Edmund Crouchback, Earl of Lancaster, but returned in a year or two as his services were more required in the Scottish wars, in which he was constantly employed up to the death of King Edward in 1307. It seems clear that, like other Marcher lords, the L'Estranges often played a part somewhat beyond their resources, and accumulated substantial debts. J. Beverley Smith comments on the meanness of Edward to those who served him. Professor Tout has suggested that this may be the reason why the branches of the family in the Marches became extinct or were absorbed into other great baronial families, while the Norfolk branch, with fewer demands on them, prospered down into the twentieth century. The Black Death may also have been a factor. Philip Ziegler in his book, *The Black Death*, records that in 1349 "John le Strange of Whitchurch" died on 20 August. He left three sons, Fulk, Humphrey and John the younger, of whom Fulk as eldest was heir. By the time the inquest was held on 30 August Fulk had already been dead two days. Before the inquisition could be held on Fulk's estate, Humphrey too was dead. John, the third brother survived but inherited a shattered estate.

CHAPTER 4.   THE 14TH CENTURY.

It was at the beginning of the 14th century that the great river down which we have been travelling with the L'Estranges with so much excitement on the Welsh border suddenly takes another great swing and, except for our interest in the branch that leads to Owain Glyn Dŵr, our ancestral story takes us back for a time to Norfolk. Before we travel in that direction we need to trace what was happening to the forebears of the Prichard and Thomas families while war and revolution were raging round them in the Marches. It is, I suppose, possible that they may have played a part in those struggles, but it seems more likely that for a period, at least, they kept out of trouble and quietly advanced the family interests. It was not only the marcher lords and Norman barons who found that the best way of doing that was by marriage. In about 1180 Cynhillin ap Rhys, the grandson of the Genillin commemorated on the font at Patricio (and like him Lord of Ystrad Yw), married Janet, daughter of Howell, Prince of Caerleon. His son married the daughter of the Lord of Upper Gwent, his great-grandson the daughter of the Lord of Cylor, Glamorgan; and his great-great-grandson, Gruffudd ap Howell, married Jannett, the daughter and heir of Gronow Ychan, Lord of Penrhos Castle. This was the marriage that really made a difference, because Penrhos Castle in South Gwent was to remain the seat of the family till late in Elizabeth's reign. Penrhos was on the banks of the Afon Llwyd just to the north of Caerleon. Gruffudd ap Howell, called Dew a Theg, the fat and handsome, was slain by Gilbert de Clare in 1282. One of the penalties of marrying families that owned castles was that there was a high risk that one would become involved in the conflicts of the marcher lords. 1282 was the year in which first Dafydd and then Llywelyn had struck against the English and in which Llywelyn was to die in the hands of the force commanded by Roger L'Estrange. Earlier in the year Gilbert de Clare had been defeated by the Welsh in south Wales and discredited in the eyes of Edward I. It must be assumed that Gruffudd had indeed become involved in the Welsh wars. I was intrigued to discover that almost 150 years earlier Gilbert de Clare's direct ancestor had been killed by the Welsh in 1135 or 1136 in the Black Mountains, an event commemorated by the Crug Dial (the Stone of Vengeance) on the Ffwddog ridge above our home. Some accounts name Iorwerth ap Owain of Caerleon as the Welshman principally responsible for the ambush. It was, I suppose, pure coincidence that Richard de Clare was killed by Welshmen from Caerleon in 1136 and almost 150 years later his direct descendant kills a Welshman from a place close to Caerleon.

Other rivulets were flowing in Wales during the half millennium between the Norman Conquest and the age of the first Elizabeth; but at first they flow through boggy ground. Ann's cousin, Julian Healing, has details of a possible Welsh branch of the Healings under the name Heylin. He has a portrait dated 1625 and a family tree that traces alleged descent from Brochwel Yskythrog (? Y scethrog), Brochwel of the tusks, Prince of Powys. I have not investigated this possible line of descent. My own forebears, the Thomas's like a large number of other south Wales families are an offshoot of the Herberts. If I was simply to go on the evidence of the family tree and a great many others like it I would confidently claim descent from "Herbert, recorded in Domesday AD 1086, as Herbert Camerarius. He was Chamberlain to William I, William II, and Henry I", and his son, "Herbert Fitz Henry, called also Herbert Fitz Herbert and 'Herbert of Winchester'," " had the living of his fathers lands in 1140" and "was Chamberlain to King Stephen and also Treasurer to that Monarch and to Henry I". Unfortunately, The Complete Peerage is dismissive of what it calls a fabricated descent; and George T. Clark in his monumental study *The Genealogies of Morgan and Glamorgan*, published in1886, tells us that "The Herberts like the Dudleys, Cecils, Spencers and Montagues-and, with all respect be it added, the family of Tudor, rose rapidly to wealth and rank at a comparatively late period of English history, and it became the business of the heralds and genealogists of a not very critical age to establish for them a pedigree----and among these apocryphal pedigrees there is none upon the proving of which more labour has been expended, or with less real result, than in the earlier parts of that of Herbert". Clark accepts that Herbert the Chamberlain was a real person; but not the subsequent chain of descent until we come to Thomas ap Adam, who came of age in 1325, and had an illegitimate son, named John or Jenkin. "The position of Jenkin is as cloudy as his ancestry. It is certain that neither he nor his son Gwilim ever held either Perthir or Werndee, of which places they are usually stated to have been lords.----Gwilim was Master Sergeant of Abergavenny in 1345. Six of Gwilim's sons founded families, and from these, and mainly from the fourth, sprung the whole race of Herbert, by whatever surname designated". For the purpose of this story, we can be content that another clearly designated river emerges from the bogs of history with Jenkin and Gwilym in the early 14th century. The Werndee referred to is an anglicised version of Wern-ddu, and a house of that name still stands on the shoulder of the Skirrid mountain a mile or two south of Abergavenny.

Professor Rees Davies confirms that the practice of referring to people as lords of the places where they lived usually had little foundation in fact: but Clarke may be wrong when he asserts that Jenkin never held Wern-ddu. If P. C. Bartrum is correct, he lived there, as did his eldest son, Philip. Bartrum also provides an interesting alternative version of the ancestry of Jenkin and Gwilym. According to him, Adam was the son of Cynhaethwy and a wife descended from Rhys Goch. His grandfather, according to this version, was Herbert of Cilleculum and his grandfather, Godwin, who died in 1199. For the purpose of this story we can leave the matter in doubt, together with other lines of descent from Jestyn ap Gwrgant (lord of Glamorgan at the time of the Conquest) referred to in the previous chapter, and be content that another clearly designated river emerges from the bogs of history with Jenkin and Gwilym in the early 14th century.

The fourth son, Thomas ap Gwilym ap Jenkin, lived at Llansaintfraed in Monmouthshire, having married Maud who was the daughter of Sir John Morley of Llansaintfraed, and died on 8th July 1348. His sister Gwenillian married one of the Prichard forbears, Meuric ap Howel Ychan of Penrhos Castle. One of the sons of Thomas ap Gwilym ap Jenkin was Sir William ap Thomas, alias Herbert, Lord of Raglan, who was knighted at Agincourt, and from whom descend the Earls of Pembroke. Sir William's youngest brother, Euan ap Thomas ap Gwilym began the line from which the Thomas family descend. The Herberts of Llanarth and Llanover who, four hundred years later will play a part in this story, descend from Howell, the third son of William ap Jenkin.

In the first decades of the 14th century, while the ancestors of the Prichards were at Penrhos Castle and Jenkin ap Adam was fathering Gwilym, the Master Sergeant of Abergavenny, Hamon L'Estrange was enfeoffed in Hunstanton by his elder brother John (VI), the second Lord Strange of Knockin. It seems clear that John (V) had been anxious to make good provision for Hamon and he therefore executed a bond, whereby he covenanted to pay a thousand marks to Hamon, or to his heirs and executors. On the fathers death in about 1309, John (VI) succeeded to the obligation, the principal security for which was the Knockin property; and as it was not convenient for him to pay up so large a sum to his brother, Hamon agreed to accept Hunstanton from his brother in full satisfaction for the debt, and when that manor was conveyed to him, he surrendered any further claim to the Knockin property. This is the moment when our branch of the L'Estrange family leave the Welsh Marches and cease their involvement in Welsh affairs. I have to say that as a Welshman I feel a sense of relief at this turn of events! The Lords Strange of Knockin continued to hold their lands on the March and the title until after nine generations Joan, the last holder of the barony, married into the family of

Lord Stanley, so that the name Strange became the courtesy title of Stanley's eldest son. After the battle of Bosworth the victorious Henry created Lord Stanley Earl of Derby. Other L'Estranges were also still involved in the affairs of Wales and the marches: in particular, Hamon's brother Eubolo was to play a vigorous role there; and there was to be one particularly curious final twist to the Welsh tale.

Elizabeth, the sister of John, Hamon and Eubolo was married in 1304 when she was only six years old to the eight year old Gruffudd ap Madog of Glyndyfrdwy, the grandfather of Owain Glyn Dŵr. John (V) was the guardian of Gruffudd during his minority. Ten years after the wedding, John's widow stated in a petition that her husband had 'bought' the marriage from Madog for £50. No doubt John was seeking to extend his family's territorial interests. Madog died in the same year as the marriage, and it was then that John became keeper of his son-in-law's lands and his guardian until his own death in 1314. The land at Glyndyfrydwy, which was in Merioneth between Corwen and Llangollen, was settled on Gruffudd and his wife Elizabeth and so in due course devolved on their grandson Owain Glyn Dŵr. The family's second estate in this part of Wales was at Sychart, very close to Knockin, and it was here that, in due course, Owain was to make his main home. Gruffudd ap Madog was in the direct male line of descent from the Princes of North Powys. His son Gruffudd Fychan ap Gruffudd served the Earl of Arundel as steward of Oswestry and acted as keeper of the lordship of Ellesmere. The family was rich, had accommodated itself readily to English rule and moved easily in the mixed society of the March. In due course Owain was to marry Margaret Hanmer, whose father was chief justice of the King's Bench, the owner of extensive estates on the North Wales border, and whose mother was Welsh.

As a young man Owain probably received legal training at the Inns of Court, and his military apprenticeship included service in the garrison at Berwick, campaigning with the King in Scotland in 1385, and taking part under the command of the Earl of Arundel in the naval victory at Cadzand in 1387. However, despite his English connection Owain's Welsh princely credentials were unimpeachable. Not only was he descended from the princes of North Powys, but through his mother, Elen, from the Lord Rhys of Deheubarth; while the line of the princes of Gwynedd had by now died out. As we turn away from Welsh affairs towards Norfolk, we thus find, only four generations after the death of Llywelyn the Last in the hands of Roger L'Estrange, the final great Welsh revolt taking place under the leadership of a man whose grand-mother was a L'Estrange.

We have seen that Hamon was enfeoffed with the manor of Hunstanton in 1309. He built the original house on a moated plateau just outside the village. (If L'Estranges had lived in Hunstanton before the move to Knockin it had only been for a short time). Beginning with Hamon, members of the family were to live in the village for the next 650 years. Six generations after Hamon, Sir Roger L'Estrange was an Esquire of the Body to Henry VII, and he was awarded his knighthood at the marriage of Arthur, the young Prince of Wales, with Katherine of Aragon in November 1501. Roger's son, John, died without an heir; and his uncle Robert's branch of the family entered into the inheritance in the person of Thomas L'Estrange, who was knighted in 1529. Born in 1494 he was betrothed in 1501 to the wealthy Anne, sister of Lord Vaux. She was born in 1494 and, clearly, this was a carefully arranged marriage by the parents of the two children.

Another interesting tributary has entered the river at this point; and if like a fisherman with a dry fly we were to follow it up stream, we would find that Anne, through her grand-mother, Lady Alice Nevill, was directly descended from John of Gaunt and Edward I. Indeed, if in the first pages of this history, I had given the same priority to the female lines as to the male, I might have begun the story not with the forebears of the Prichard and L'Estrange families, but with Alfred the Great! The blood of the Saxon kings that includes two Edwards, two Edmunds, Edgar, and Ethelread the Unready flows via St Margaret of Scotland to Matilda, the wife of Henry I. The Empress Matilda, by this time the wife of Geofrey of Anjou, carries it by way of their son, Henry II, and five other English kings to John of Gaunt, enriched by the genes of their wives, among them Eleanor of Aquitaine, Eleanor of Castille, and Isabella of France. Henry I introduced the blood of the Dukes of Normandy and William the Conqueror into the flood.

Katherine Swynford was the mistress of John of Gaunt. Their daughter, Joan of Gaunt, fell in love with and married Ralph, 1st Earl of Westmorland. She was legitimised by Royal proclamation with the condition that none of her descendants should have the right to the throne. She and Ralph were the parents of Alice, Countess of Salisbury, and grandparents of Alice Nevill. Again, following the various tributaries upstream from Ann Vaux and her mother, Elizabeth Fitzhugh, we find Fitzhughs, Willoughby de Eresbys and St Quintins, and also a batch of Earls: Salisbury, Surrey, Arundel and Westmorland, together with the fifth Lord Strange. One is irresistibly reminded of a Shakespeare play as one reads this roll call. Indeed John of Gaunt, his son-in-law the Earl of Salisbury, and Lord Willoughby are all characters in *King Richard II*. The game of descent from John of Gaunt can be played by a great many families and a similar tributary flows down to eventually feed the Prichard stream in Glamorgan.

Thomas L'Estrange was a key figure in the history of the family. He is the subject of a chalk drawing at Windsor by Hans Holbein the younger, made during his first visit to the English Court in 1526-8 (a copy of which is at Pont Esgob Mill) and of a later portrait in oils based on the drawing painted in 1536. Thomas's life represents a junction point where the history of the family begins to divide between the Norfolk and the Irish branches, as he was the ancestor to both. He was an Esquire of the Body to King Henry VIII and was present at the Field of the Cloth of Gold in 1520 and at Henry's marriage to Ann Boleyn, and in 1536 'to the dethe of the Queen', apparently to witness her execution. He was Sheriff of Norfolk in 1530 and after this date was permanently resident in the county where he substantially added to his properties and wealth, partly by judicious acquisitions of leases and lands from monastic superiors before their houses were dissolved. The lives of husband and wife are exceptionally well documented because of the remarkable survival of a substantial L'Estrange archive (now in the Norfolk Record Office). The biographical entry in the ONDB explains that the documents record in fascinating detail how Thomas made and spent his money; what the family ate; how they entertained themselves and others; and how they played their respective roles as prominent landowners in Norfolk. Thomas was under the patronage of the Duke of Norfolk and was closely connected with Henry's Secretary of State during the 1530s, Thomas Cromwell; and played his part as an official in dealing with local disturbances that occurred in the troubled period that followed the dissolution of the monasteries He was buried on the north side of the chancel of Hunstanton church on 17th January 1545.

We now discover another river, because in the very same year, 1533, that Thomas L'Estrange was attending the wedding of Henry VIII and Ann Boleyn, Sir Edward Burgh died. He was the first of the four husbands of Katharine Parr, Henry's last and only surviving wife. His death and that of an older brother, Thomas, meant that William, the third son, became the fourth Lord Burgh. The first Lord Burgh, or Borough (of Gainsborough in Lincolnshire) was summoned as a Baron by writ in 1487. In 1455 he had succeeded to the estates of his Percy mother who was a great-grand-daughter of the first Earl of Northumberland. The fifth Lord Burgh took his seat in 1584 and became Lord Deputy of Ireland in 1597. The sixth Lord Burgh was only three years old when he died in 1597 and the barony fell into abeyance. The co-heirs were his four sisters, one of whom, Frances, married a Francis Coppinger. They had a son, Nicholas, and a grandson also called Francis, whose daughter, Susanna, was to marry David Thomas, an event about which we shall hear more in a later chapter.

CHAPTER 5.   THE TUDOR PERIOD.

With the reign of Henry VIII we have now arrived at a momentous period in the history of our ancestors when the L'Estrange river takes yet another great turn, this time to Ireland, and other new streams suddenly emerge to change the landscape. In Yorkshire the Brooke family makes its first appearance. Roger Brooke was living in 1512 and died in 1521. His son John Brooke of Holme founded the family woollen business in 1541. In Wales the Prichard family establish themselves at Llanover; the Thomas family becomes prominent in Glamorgan; and the Coppinger's, who later marry into the Thomas's, arrive in another tributary. Tempting as it is to look at the new streams, whilst Thomas L'Estrange is still fresh in our minds, we will stay for a while longer with the L'Estranges, because it is his sons Nicholas, Richard, and Thomas, who take us to Ireland.

Sir Nicholas L'Estrange (1511-1580) succeeded his father as lord of Hunstanton in 1545. Quite early in his career he entered the service of the Dukes of Norfolk. He was first elected a Member of Parliament in 1547. He was knighted by Somerset, the Lord Protector, during the Scottish campaign of 1547. He was accused of conspiring with the rebels during Kett's rebellion in 1549. He briefly disappeared from the political scene during the reign of Mary; but he re-emerged as M.P. for King's Lynn in 1555; and he subsequently sat for the Duke of Norfolk's pocket borough of Castle Rising. He nearly lost his life after being arrested because of his alleged involvement with Thomas Howard's moves towards an attempted marriage with Mary Queen of Scots. Thomas Howard, the fourth Duke of Norfolk, went to the block; but Sir Nicholas survived, although he lost his seat on the Commission of the Peace in 1571. In was probably then that he joined Richard who was already in Ireland, where he was known as Sir Nicholas L'Estrange of Athleague. However he returned to Norfolk after some years, was restored to the bench and died in 1580. The Athleague property may have been first acquired by Sir Thomas L'Estrange whose life was chronicled in the previous chapter; and Richard, his second son, may have been sent out to manage it. Richard is the ancestor of the Moystown or Irish branch of the family. However, the great bulk of the Irish properties were acquired by Richard's younger brother, Thomas. Cord Oestmann in his book about the L'Estrange family and its Norfolk estates, *Lordship and Community*, gives the names of six sons of Sir

Thomas of Hunstanton (although admitting that the exact number of his children are not known, a rather curious fact bearing in mind the detailed records that survive about the family). The Thomas who now made such a mark in Ireland must have been one of those sons. He acquired his estates, principally in County Roscommon and County Westmeath, by purchase from the native Irish, confirmed afterwards by the crown in different ways. Some of these confirmations came after Thomas's death when the property rights of his successors came under challenge. There are a number of examples of these in the Patent and Close Rolls of Elizabeth, notably leases of the priory of Loughsewedy and its adjacent land, originally had from the crown in 1566.

The Irish Sir Thomas, who died in 1590, is mentioned repeatedly in the Irish State Papers of the reign of Elizabeth as a most efficient servant of the crown. Sir H. Sidney, leaving him in charge of the Province of Connaught, speaks of him as 'learned in the law'; and he appears also to have been a military leader peculiarly adapted to service in Ireland. His first recorded service is described 'coming with his Kerne to the siege of the Castle of Meelick by water with great ordnance'. In January 1559, being the "Captain of Athlone" and residing at Loughsewedy in the County of Westmeath, he was appointed 'Sheriff of Westmeath during pleasure' and in April 1562 was one of the 'commissioners of Martial Law for the County of Westmeath, Connaught, and all other Irish Counties near the same on both sides of the Shannon'. When Bingham, Governor of Connaught, was given leave of absence and sent to Holland, the Queen named Sir Thomas to act during his absence. In 1583 he was admitted to the Irish Privy Council and in 1585 he received his Knighthood. He died at 'Galway on the first Thursday in Lent 1590 and that was a great calamity for there was not in Connaught a foreigner more to be deplored by Connaught than he'. He married Margaret Bathe, the mother of his step-son Francis, afterwards Sir Francis Shean. He had no children of his own; and it appears that it was from him that the Lordship of Athleague passed to his great-nephew Sir Nicholas L'Estrange who had inherited Hunstanton from his brother Thomas. Sir Nicholas died in1591 only a year after the 'Captain of Athlone', and his son Sir Hamon sold the Irish property that he had inherited to John Jay or Gay of Halveston in Norfolk. However, John Jay was the brother-in-law and probably the trustee of Thomas "FitzRichard L'Estrange", the grandson of the original Richard, which no doubt was a factor in the transactions affecting the various Irish properties now in the hands of the L'Estrange family. While Richard L'Estrange, the founder of the Irish branch, seems to have been principally at Athleague, his eldest son Hamon appears to have settled on the Castle Strange or County Roscommon Estate. Thomas FitzRichard exchanged these estates for those at Moystown in Kings County in 1633 and the family was to live there for more than two hundred years.

Having thus established the L'Estranges at Moystown, it is time to turn our attention to the Brookes in Yorkshire. The reign of Henry VIII saw the emergence of a new river that was to flow broad and strong for more than four hundred years. If the L'Estranges had been characteristic representatives of mediaeval Britain, the Brooke family in Yorkshire would through eighteen generations represent trade, in due course the growth of a middle class, and the development of a modern commercial world. Roger Brooke of Holme, south of Huddersfield is first heard of in 1512 and died in 1521. It is, I believe because of him that my first name is Roger. That first, Roger, must have seen most of the reign of Henry VII and may well have been alive during the reigns of Edward IV, Edward V and Richard III. His son, John, founded the family woollen business in 1541, six years before the death of Henry VIII and seven years before his own death. John Brooke and Sons is almost certainly the oldest family firm in Britain; and, what is even more remarkable, it has gone in unbroken succession from father to son from the reign of Henry VIII to the start of the new millennium in the reign of Elizabeth II.

G. M. Trevelyan has written that "The history of the change from mediaeval to modern England might well be written in the form of a social history of the English cloth trade." Before the reign of Edward III England had exported wool to the looms of Flanders and Italy. Trevelyan describes how under the patronage of Edward, the first Flemish weavers brought their skill to this island: "the gift of their skill became a national treasure, destined to multiply a thousand-fold. The French and Flemish Huguenots who flocked over in Elizabethan and Stuart times -----were no less helpful than their mediaeval forerunners in developing ever new branches of the English weaving industry". Yorkshire was one of a number of rural areas that rapidly followed the example of East Anglia which was greatly enriched in the Fifteenth and Sixteenth Centuries by the cloth trade.

The first Brooke mill was built beside the swift flowing river Holme, near the village of the same name; but later the business moved a few miles down the valley to Armitage Bridge, where there was more land and more water to power the wheels and later a massive turbine. Within a hundred years of its beginning two Johns, two Rogers and a Humphrey, had established a tradition in which the eldest son remained in the business and built on the success of earlier generations. In many families the urge to leave the business and become landed gentry fatally weakened the entrepreneurial spirit and led to the speedy decline of the enterprise. In later times there were to be a good many Brookes who did become landed gentry, clergymen, aesthetes, travellers and empire builders; but for more than four hundred years enough of the Brooke manpower and money remained in the business to ensure its continuing success. The heads of the family did not neglect the trappings of wealth, but lived in large houses in the valley, where water power generated affluence.

In the age of the Tudors, when the Brookes were establishing themselves by the river Holme in Yorkshire and the L'Estranges were acquiring extensive properties in Ireland, the Prichards and the Thomases were becoming landed gentry in south Wales. We know that Ievan ap Meuric of Penrhos Castle was alive in 1493. His younger son Howel ap Ievan married Jane, the heiress of Llanover and as a consequence became Lord of Llanover, where the family was to live for several generations. Howel's great-grandson, William ap Richard, was the first to style himself Prichard. Like his great-grandfather he married an heiress, the daughter of Watkin ap Hugh of Killurch. He was burried at Llanover where his memorial brass is still to be seen, inscribed:

Here lyeth the bodies of William Prichard of Llanover and of Mathew Prichard of Llanover, his sonne and heir, lineally descended from the bodye of Cradock Vraich, Earl of Hereford and Prince between Wye and Severn.

Mathew's son, bearing the same name, was High Sheriff of Monmouth in 1596 and he died in 1622. His wife, Sissylt, was the daughter of Edward Lewis of the Vann, Glamorgan who was High Sheriff there in 1548, 1555, and 1559. His younger brother, Charles, was Vicar of Llanover and another brother, Valentine, was also High Sheriff of Monmouthshire in 1609 and a J.P. It is clear that by now the family was playing a prominent part in the public affairs of the county.

The Thomas family were performing similar roles in Glamorgan. James Thomas of Michaelstone near Cowbridge was Sheriff for Glamorgan in 1550. His eldest son, John Thomas of Llanvihangel was Sheriff in 1578: a younger brother James became Chester Herald at Arms, created by the Earl of Leicester in 1587; and a sister, Jane, produced a son who was created Baron Hervey of Kidbrooke in 1628. William Hervey was an interesting person. He distinguished himself in the defeat of the Spanish Armada in1588; was knighted by the Earl of Essex at Cadiz in 1596 and served under that commander in the naval expedition against Cadiz in 1597. He took a leading part in the Irish wars. It was apparently he who was the William Hervey, M.P. for Horsham 1601, and for Petersfield 1604-11. He was created a Baronet in 1619, and Baron Hervey of Rosse, county Wexford, in 1620 and finally Baron Hervey of Kidbrooke. The suggestion has been made that he was the W.H. to whom Shakespeare's Sonnets were dedicated.

Our branch of the family is descended from James, the Chester Herald. The Rev. Robert Thomas who was born between 1565 and 1570 was Rector of Coychurch for more than 50 years. He is buried in the chancel of the church there, as is his eldest son Edward who was born in 1598 and died in 1645.

G. M. Trevelyan again provides a useful commentary on the social revolution in which the family was caught up. "The leading class in England was the landed gentry or squires. They were no longer a feudal or a military class, and when civil war broke out in 1642 had to be taught the art of soldiery from the beginning. As far as it is possible to define the important and recognised distinction between 'gentle' and 'simple' in the new England, the 'gentleman' was a landowner who could show a coat of arms, and who had the right when he wished it to wear a rapier and challenge to a duel any other 'gentleman' from a Duke downwards ----The squires or smaller country gentry acquired a new importance under the Tudors. It was not merely that many of them had purchased the monastic lands at an easy rate. They were in a new social position, because the Barons and Abbots who had lorded it over them so long had been brought low. They themselves, whether as Ministers of the Crown or as local Justices of the Peace, became the mainstay of the government, the leaders of the House of Commons, the real rulers of the countryside. It was the squires, principally, who in the Stuart era led both the Cavalier and the Roundhead party". C. V. Wedgwood in The King's Peace, writing about the reign of Charles I, suggests that things may have been rather different in Wales. "The gentry of Wales were as a rule poorer and simpler than the gentry of England. 'You can sooner find fifty gentlemen of £100 a year than five of £500,' recorded an observer from England, or, as a traditional jingle put it of one Welsh county:

> Alas, alas, poor Radnorshire,
> Never a park, nor ever a deer,
> Nor ever a squire of five hundred a year
> Save Sir Richard Fowler of Abbey Cwm Hir.

But the Welsh gentleman in his stone-built farmhouse, with salmon hanging in the smoke of his chimney, a dresser with wooden trenchers upon it, fixed benches round the fire and about the walls, and a woven cloth for the parlour table on a Sunday, lived a traditional and patriarchal life among servants and tenantry who looked upon him as something more than an employer and landlord and felt for him and his a tribal loyalty and pride. Often he still did not trouble himself to have an English surname; knowing well by oral tradition that he was descended from royal stock, he scorned the English insistence on family names; himself he was David Evans; his son, called Evan, from his grandfather, would be Evan Davis. His life, impoverished reflection of the Celtic tradition, had a simplicity and poetry of its own, but even in its decadence Celtic society was more rigid than the competitive, make-your-own-way society of England".

Monmouthshire was even then more English and more prosperous than Radnorshire, and its squires, like those in Glamorgan, were probably nearer to the English pattern than those in Radnorshire; but the fact that William was the first to use a surname in the English style and call himself Prichard suggests that things were only changing slowly and that life there was still characteristic of the border or the march, with many features borrowed from the countries on either side of it.

So far we have identified rivers and smaller tributaries rising in East Anglia, the Welsh Marches, Glamorgan and Ireland. In Scotland the burns rising amid bogs and heather are even harder to detect than south of the border; but it was probably during the reign of Elizabeth I, or rather of Mary Queen of Scots and James VI of Scotland, that the McLeans first appear in the story. There are documents concerning landed property that provide the evidence. Some family histories start with Allan McLean of Shuna who became the owner of Shuna in 1674 when he acquired the lands of Shuna from Lord Neill Campbell; but details of a contract made in 1648 refers to both Allan's great-great grandfather, Sorley, and his great-grand father, Allan. Archibald, the son of Allan McLean of Shuna settled on Islay and by doing so introduced a fascinating new element into our tale. Although we have to wait until the end of the 18th century for that wee burn to become a raging torrent this is the place to refer to the battle fought at Traigh Gruinart by a McLean ancestor whose grave Ann and I sought and found on one of our Islay visits. An account of the battle is given in a pamphlet, *Reminiscences of Islay* by W. N. Blair published in 1983.

"Among the minor troubles of the Macdonalds was a long standing feud with the Macleans. After various questionable transactions on both sides, the quarrel terminated in a pitched battle at Traigh Gruinart. Sir Lachlan MacLean of Duart, who had invaded Islay with a large force, was met by his nephew, Sir James Macdonald, and a bloody conflict ensued. Before leaving Mull, Lachlan had consulted a witch as to the issue of the expedition. She warned him not to land on a Thursday, nor to drink out of a certain well at Gruinart. But, like other people, he did the things that he ought not to have done, and left undone those things that he ought to have done; so, in the day of battle, there was no strength in him. Lachlan's army was defeated, and he and three hundred of his followers were left dead on the field. The Chief is believed to have been killed by an arrow shot from the bow of a little man called Ddu Sith--- Black Fairy. This worthy, who had no sympathies either way, first offered his services to the MacLeans. Lachlan Mor, himself a giant, refused the offer with scorn, saying he would not have such a pigmy in his ranks. This raised the ire of little Ddu Sith, who straight-way transferred his services to the Macdonalds. He planted himself in a milk white thorn that grew convenient to the field of strife, and made Lachlan Mor his target. After the battle, Sir Lachlan's foster mother was removing his remains from the field on a sledge. She was accompanied by a young lad, her own son. The vehicle was too small for the giant body of the chief, and the contortions to which it was subjected brought a smile to the face of the youth. Such disrespect to the "mighty slain" was too much for the faithful Highland nurse, and she instantly avenged it by plunging a dirk into the heart of her own child, killing him on the spot."

Two other tributaries emerge in Ireland at the end of the 16th or early in the 17th centuries which in due time were to merge and contribute richly to the story. Nicholas Barnewall, the son and heir of Sir Patrick Barnewall from County Dublin was in 1646 created Baron of Turvey and Viscount Barnewall of Kingsland. In June 1645 he was in prison, being charged with complicity in a plot against the Lord Protector, by whom his property had been sequestrated. However, it was restored to him in 1660. In 1617 he married Bridget, the daughter of the Earl of Kildare and his wife, Frances, who was the daughter of Charles Howard, Earl of Nottingham. They had a daughter, Mary, from whom descend the family of Colclough who had settled in Ireland during the reign of Edward III and who were to perform roles in this play during a later act. They had a son, Frances, whose daughter, Mary, married Dudley Colclough. The Colclough's son, Caesar, was M.P. for Wexford, and his great-granddaughter, Harriet, married Lt-Colonel Jonas Watson who, as we shall hear, was to play an heroic role in the Irish rebellion of 1798.

CHAPTER 6.   THE CIVIL WAR AND AFTER.

It was the Civil War that provided the setting for the next turbulence in the family story. Our ancestors fought on different sides. Henry L'Estrange of Moystown in the King's County in Ireland was a Parliament Officer who was one of those who received the surrender of the Royalist Army of Connaught. On the opposite side William Prichard of Llanover and Goytre was ruined paying the fines of the Royalist prisoners after the Civil War and as a result was forced to sell the estate of Llanover. His name was on the Address to Cromwell signed in 1655. His younger brother, Thomas, who was born in 1599 was a Captain in the army of Charles I, as apparently was Jenkyn Prichard about whom we will hear more in a moment. Our own direct ancestor, the youngest son, Benjamin, after the destruction of Raglan Castle went into voluntary exile during the Commonwealth, but at the Restoration he returned to Goytre within the Llanover manor which remained in the family until early in the 18th century. These were exciting times.

Benjamin's son, William, lived at Goytre and died there in 1722; but his son, also called William, sold Goytre (the last remaining part of the Llanover estate in the hands of the family) in about 1730 to Charles Hanbury Williams and went to live at the Hill, Trostrey. He died in 1755. His portrait is now at the home of my cousin William Prichard in Monmouthshire. The only son of the William who sold Goytre, yet another William, was baptised there in 1718, settled in Chepstow in 1747 and died there in 1795. The youngest of his three sons was called Thomas, from whom our branch of the family descend.

Sir Joseph Bradney in *A History of Monmouthshire,* vol 1, part 2b, (first published in 1906) denies the existence of William and his brothers, Thomas and Benjamin, or at any rate refuses to acknowledge that they were the sons of Matthew Prichard of Llanover and his wife Sissylt. According to Bradney, "Barbara, only child and heir of Matthew Prichard, married about 1620 Walter Rumsey of Usk, a Welsh judge, and took the estate to her husband." Bradney dismisses the evidence produced by The Rev. Thomas Gregory Smart in *The Genealogy of Descendants of Prichard* that convincingly shows that Bradney was wrong, but provides no good reasons for doing so. Smart was himself a Prichard descendant, and he relied on the researches of The Rev. R. Neville who held the Rectory of Goytre from 1738 to 1742, together with those of a successor, The Rev. Thomas Evans, who (together with The Rev. Joshua Evans, Vicar of Llanover) issued a signed document setting out the results of his enquiries in August 1866. Evans concluded that Matthew Prichard left behind him three sons, William, Jenkyn (John) and Benjamin, together with a daughter, Barbara. He states that Barbara married *circa* 1606 Judge Walter Rumsey, who, in the year 1628 acquired property in Llanover which had belonged to the Springet family; and that in 1631 Rumsey was entered in the Court Leet records as having become possessed of part ("a messuage") of the Prichard property at Llanover. At the same date, the eldest son, Matthew William Prichard was entered in more than one place as still holding Llanover property. Evans had searched the manorial records of the manor of Pelleney in the parish of Goytre and found detailed records of properties held by various members of the Prichard family; and on the basis of the facts that he had established, he concluded that "Mr Neville, my predecessor at Goytre from 1738 to 1742, was correct in the account of the issue of Matthew Prichard, of Llanover, which was by him sent to Thomas Prichard, son of William, and grandson of Jenkyn, the second son of Matthew".

The circumstances in which Neville's letter was written in 1738 is relevant. The tradition of the family is that after the destruction of Raglan, Benjamin suffered voluntary exile during the Commonwealth, and at the Restoration, he, or his son, obtained the estate known as the Manor House of Goytre (now the Church Farm). According to Neville, during the Civil War period the heir of the elder brother, Jenkyn, made no claim to the family properties. It is possible that Captain Jenkyn Prichard had perished in the Civil War. In 1646 he had sent his infant son, William, to Chorley in Lancashire "to avoid the accidents and dangers of civil war". A grandson of Jenkyn believed that he was entitled to the Goytre property which by then was in the possession of Benjamin's son, William. The destruction of registers and wills, and the disappearance of the manorial records of Abergavenny made it impossible for him to produce any legal documents to substantiate the claim, but prompted the long letter from The Rev. R. Neville setting out the family history, a copy of which was kept by another family member. This manuscript recorded that "The ancient family of the Prichards were possessed of Llanover Court in the County of Monmouth, for many years past, and held great possessions there and in adjacent villages". Neville, in order to confirm that Jenkyn had been a Captain in the King's army and other facts about the family "had made enquiry of the Vicar, and Churchwardens, and others likely to be informed".

I suppose it is possible that Barbara brought as her dowry to her marriage to Rumsey the house called Ty mawr or Ty uchaf where to-day Llanover House stands, while her brothers continued to live at Llanover Court or Goytre. Confusion on the subject is easy to explain because, if we take the story back several generations, we discover that the Prichards owned a number of properties in the area. The William Prichard recorded in the memorial brass in Llanover church lived at Llanover Court. In 1566 his son, Matthew, is entered in the manorial records as holding lands and a house in the manor of Pelleney (Goytre) by inheritance, and lands and the Curt y Porthir in Llanover, together with a house at Rhydymeirch, the hamlet in what is now the village of Llanover just up the little stream from Ty Mawr. Archdeacon Coxe, writing his well known *Tour of Monmouthshire* in Llanover House in 1801, states that the Prichards "were succeeded by the Rumseys, who, unable to derive their origin from a knight of the round table, and a companion of King Arthur, yet yielded unwillingly the palm of descent to their predecessors". That comment, however dubious in its historical claim, hardly suggest that he believed that Llanover had come by inheritance from a Prichard sole heir!

The old Manor House at Goytre, now Church Farm, in which our forbears lived is still there close to the church. The Gwent/Monmouthshire volume of the *Buildings of Wales* (Pevsner), edited by John Newman, described Church Farm as *"A good group, the three-bay c17 house unusually formed, with three-storeyed gable and windows under hoodmoulds symmetrically disposed below it. Original central doorway and door, protected by a delightful rustic c18 columned porch. The windows themselves are c18 casements. Unaltered barn adjoining to the r, with central porch and prentice roofs"*. Sadly, the barn now has a corrugated roof, but the group is still charming. Apart from the 18c refinements it cannot have changed much since our family lived there after the Civil War.

Down in Glamorgan Thomas Thomas (born in 1628) was not, as far as I know, involved in the Civil War; but he had to flee from Wales because of a duel

Steams that rise in the same valley and flood plain sometimes meander and rejoin each other. At this point it is of some interest to carry the story of the Llanover property forward far into the future. Llanover was acquired by the Waddington family. In 1823 Augusta the daughter of Benjamin Waddington of Llanover married Benjamin Hall, who was to become a Liberal M.P., First Commissioner of Public Works (passing his name on to 'Big Ben') and Baron Llanover of Llanover and Abercarn. Lady Llanover became famous for a passionate and somewhat overdone espousal of all things Welsh. Their daughter, Charlotte, married John Arthur Edward Jones of Llanarth, who in 1848 changed the family name to Herbert. As a result Llanover became the property of the Herberts. The Jones's were the descendants of Howell, the third son of Gwilym ap Jenkin, the same Gwilym ap Jenkin who was the forebear of the Thomas family (by the fourth son, Thomas) and the Earls of Pembroke, together with the other grander Herberts. While the Thomas branch were content with their name, the Jones branch were not. It is alleged that when Mr Jones of Llanarth politely asked Lord Pembroke, the head of the Herbert family, whether he had any objection to the proposed change, he replied that he had none, but that if every other Jones in Wales was going to follow suit with a similar application, he (Lord Pembroke) would seriously have to consider the advisability of changing his own name from Herbert to Jones! John Arthur Edward Herbert's son became Baron Treowen and died without an heir. His younger brother, Sir Arthur Herbert of Llanarth, was the grandfather of Robin Herbert and great-grand father of Elizabeth who has inherited Llanover.

In Ireland, Henry L'Estrange, The Parliament Officer's will was dated 20 January 1665. He was to be buried within the church of Tesarane. The considerable list of properties referred to in the will, which were to go to his son Tom (known to the family as Old Tom) and his heirs male, indicates how successful the family had been in acquiring land at Castle Strange, at Moystown, in the Barony of Longford in Galway, in Kilkenny, and in other places in the King's County. A memo states that Henry on the day of his death and after making his will told his brother William of Castle Cuffe that it was his will that when his eldest son was 21, if he was then thought by the executors "to be capable for the management of a great estate", he should be allowed additional moneys for maintenance out of the estate. Curiously his eldest son who is referred to as Thomas in the main part of the will is referred to as Hamon in the memo. Presumably the nine year old boy was known by both those family names. Old Tom (or Hamon) was still alive in 1732 and his son, William, was to die before him. We know little about William but we know more about old Tom's grandson, 'Handsome Harry', because a splendid portrait of him that is still in the ownership of the family.

Two other great rivers which were to add to the flood now emerge. Jonas Watson, of Lampford, Essex, saw a son of the same name baptised in the year that he died, 1663. He was to play an important role in the history of the British Army. In Gloucestershire, we know that John Healing who died in 1702 was alive in 1661. We will hear much more about the Healings in due course.

Three foreign streams also joined their waters in the flood. Jacobus von Rhenen arrived in the Cape of Good Hope from East Prussia in 1725. Our Huguenot ancestors arrived in Ireland in 1689; and later, in 1786, Nathaniel Wallich was born in Copenhagen. The first faint meanderings of a river in France that produced our Huguenot ancestors can be found back in the late 15th century. When Josias de Champagné, in order to claim exemptions to certain taxes to which the *noblesse* were entitled had, because of an order in Council of 1667, to establish that his ancestors had born appropriate titles since before 1560, he was able to do so; and he proved by documentary evidence descent from one Jean Roillard who purchased a property near Blois in 1482. The wife of Josias, Marie de la Rochefoucauld, was a member of one of the younger branches of that great family, and it would appear that she was a descendant of the first Count de la Rochefoucauld, who died in 1517, and grand-daughter of Charles, Duc de la Rochfoucault. However, I propose to take up the story in 1667 when Josias de Robillard, Chevalier, Seigneur de Champagné, married Marie de Rochefoucauld. Both couples were large landowners and both were Huguenots, but they differed greatly in character. In a paper written for his children Josias explains in clear and moderate language the grounds of his adherence to the reformed religion; but he seems to have been weak in health and character. Thomas Le Fanu, from whose contributions to the Huguenot Society's proceedings, my knowledge of the subject is drawn, comments: "Making every allowance for the difficulties which he had to face, there is a striking difference between his readiness to accept the view that he must give up either his faith or his family and his wife's determination to preserve both". Those difficulties mounted in the years between their marriage and the revocation of the Edict of Nantes in 1685. The Edict had permitted the holding of divine worship according to the rites of the reformed religion in the manor-houses of lordships such as those held by Josias and Marie de Champagné. Decrees of 1681 and 1682 alarmed many Protestants and compelled all who had families or lands to look carefully into their position. They were faced with the alternative of lapsing or seeing their children lapse from their faith if they remained in France, or of losing their property if they emigrated. In a letter which he wrote to his children in 1686, Josias explained the dilemma that he faced (this is a translation from the original).

My pretended adoption of the Roman Catholic religion will doubtless surprise you my dear children, as well as those who shall have read the letter I addressed to you from Paris the 15th July 1685-----as the act may be interpreted unfavourably and cause scandal to my relations, I think it is a duty in order to stop its circulation to declare the reason which obliged me to do so, and to confess all my criminal proceedings, and at the same time the good intentions which God by His Grace preserved in my heart during this grievous event. At the end of the month of last September 1685 the Attorney General of Limoges sent for me in great haste, three times in one week, to inform me in the name of the King that I should change my religion, and after long conferences which I had on that subject with the King, the Bishop and a few Friars, seeing that I could not be convinced by their arguments he sent (Marechal de Logis) 24 Dragoons back with written orders to remain with me until my conversion and that of my family took place. Soon after the Captain and his band was added, and gave orders to fortify the garrison occasionally and also to threaten to separate my family from me. It is true that seeing the storm raging all over France and that it carried off nearly all the Protestants of both Town and Country and especially those of the neighbourhood of Saintognes when more than forty gentlemen of that Province had all of a sudden (having assembled together) changed their religion or had pledged their word to do so on very distressing conditions, I thought my only resource was to try and escape alone to a foreign country and thus abandon my family, or enter into an agreement for the sake of my children to enable us to avoid Cloisters and prisons and to be able to put our persons and consciences in a place of safety. I confess that paternal affection obliged me to adopt this resolution and to sign the writing the copy of which is as follows:- "I the undersigned declare that in obedience to the wishes of the King I adopt the Roman Catholic religion and adhere to the pure doctrine taught in it conformable to the Doctrine of Our Lord Jesus Christ and His Holy Apostles, promise to adore and serve God as He ought to be adored and served and not in any other way and remaining of my own accord to the worship which is due to Him". He goes on to explain *"I thought I might sign that writing for the sake of my children to screen them and myself from the storm because my promise only engaged me to adore and serve God as he ought to be adored and served--however the threat which afterwards they persisted in holding out to me of taking my children from me forced me to go to Mass---".* Josias had persuaded himself that he could sign the somewhat ambiguous document with good conscience, but the authorities had then taken steps to make him a convert in practice and not merely in name.

Marie did not follow her husband's example. Women were often harder to convert than men; but it soon became evident that she must either leave her home at Bernerè or attend mass. She therefore moved into La Rochelle, which was only ten or twelve miles from properties belonging to her husband. She had with her three sons and four daughters. She remained there until the spring of 1687 when she escaped. Her own account of her adventures and those of her family is very vivid.

"10 April 1687 my four daughters and my youngest sons with my cousin de Masiriee went out of La Rochelle at night. They broke open a hogshead of wine, which they threw into the sea, and they were concealed in its place. It was only a vessel of 18 tons. They gave 1200 francs. I had gone to the country for my confinement. I left it on the 23rd of June and betook myself to La Rochelle. The departure of my children was very secret and it would be too long to describe all the tricks I was obliged to have resource to hide them; I kept myself very secretly at La Rochelle, always concealed until the 2nd of July. During that time I had no opportunity of getting on board a ship. I travelled one night with my eldest son and my maid servant four leagues on foot, the second night during which by the Grace of God I travelled two more took us to the ship which was three leagues out

at sea at the foot of the citadel de Rei. We were put in the bottom of the hold on some salt where we remained eight days at anchor well hid. They made a search without finding us. We set sail and arrived at Falmouth eight days afterwards It was not without fear and much risk. The English and the refugees of the locality received us delightfully coming forward to meet us and doing many other kind things. It appeared to us as if we came from what is called Purgatory and arrived in Paradise.----".

From Falmouth they went on first to Exeter and then to Rotterdam. Marie spent some time in The Hague where she had an audience with the Princess of Orange. Josias escaped in June 1688. After the Prince of Orange had set off to take the throne of England, Josias was appointed a Captain under the Colonelcy of M de Cravenour, a Dutch nobleman, and in 1689 was placed under the command of the Duke of Schomberg in Ireland. He sailed on the mail from Chester to rejoin his regiment; but was taken ill in Belfast and died in October 1689.

Marie who had, with her husband, enjoyed large estates, two country houses and a cottage near the seaside was now living with her children in a poorly furnished suburban house. Her capital was estimated by her eldest son, Josias, in 1722 at £3000 and she had a small pension first granted by King William in 1690. She remained in Holland until 1722 when Josias took her to his home at Portarlington in Ireland where she died in 1730. Josias had been born at Champagné in March 1673 and was twelve years old at the date of the Revocation. After he had escaped with his mother from France he lived with her for two years and at one time hoped to secure a position as a page to Princess Mary. That hope was frustrated by the elevation of William and Mary to the English throne because of the impossibility of giving such a post to a foreigner.

After the death of his father in 1689 Josias became an ensign in Isaac de la Meloniere's French regiment of foot in the Duke of Schomberg's army in Ireland. With the regiment he took part in the Battle of the Boyne as well as engagements in Athlone and at Aughrim; and he went on to fight in Flanders in 1692. In 1695 the King, prompted by the Compte de Soissons, brother of Prince Eugene, gave him a commission in the regiment commanded by a Colonel John Tidcomb (which later became the 14th (Prince of Wales's Own) West Yorkshire Regiment), which after serving in Flanders was sent to Ireland. As a result of an Act passed in 1698 it became necessary for Josias de Champagné to be naturalised if he was to stay in the British Army and receive his pay, and he became a British citizen in 1698. In 1705 he married Lady Jane Forbes, the second daughter of the second Earl of Granard. Soon after his marriage Josias and Jane settled in Portarlington, a settlement of French Officers established by Henry de Ruigny, Earl of Galway and built a house in

King Street on some plots that he had acquired. After some further years on the Active list he went on half pay in 1715. Despite the financial problems that he faced as a consequence, he seems to have fared reasonably well by the quite modest standards of the Portarlington community. In 1714 he had acquired under lease 115 acres outside the town in addition to the three town plots that he held. He had a fine garden with grounds running down to the river together with land on the opposite bank and a boat so that he could get to it.

His son, Arthur, was born at Portarlington in October 1714, his godfathers being Arthur, Earl of Granard and his mother's cousin Arthur, Earl of Donegal. Josias died in 1737. Arthur won a scholarship to Trinity College, Dublin in 1734; and was admitted to priest's orders in 1740. Le Fanu tells us that he "performed his duties diligently according to the standard of the day, but that standard was low. He was a pluralist and frankly Erastian in his view of Church government. He explains to his cousins in Germany that preferments in the Church of Ireland are the gift of the King, and that he or his Viceroy disposes them to those who can make the best interest and get themselves best recommended". In 1741 he obtained the rectories of Monasteroris and Castropetre, which included the town of Edenberry. He also held the vicarages of Muuingar and Kilclonfert, but entrusted the work of those parishes to curates. His mother died in 1760 and the following year he was appointed Dean of Clonmacnoise. He died at Portarlington in 1800. He had married Marianne, the daughter of Colonel Isaac Hamon in 1745, and had twelve children, six sons and six daughters.

His eldest daughter, Jane became the Countess of Uxbridge whose eldest son was Field-Marshall Henry William Paget, first Marquis of Anglesey ('One Leg.') who commanded the British cavalry at Waterloo. His second daughter Letitia, who was born in 1748, married George Stepney of Durrow Abbey, Queen's County in 1767. Their son, Lt-Col Herbert Rawson Stepney married Alicia L'Estrange, and in due course their daughter, Louisa Vicentia Rawson Stepney, married George Burdett L'Estrange, Ann's great-great-grandfather, who will later play a big part in this story.

While in France in April 2001 Ann and I stayed with friends in Boisse and visited La Rochelle, 42 km to the west. This was the port from which Josias and Marie fled. We also went to the village of Champagné, south of Rochefort, in the hope that it was the place from which the family took its name. There is in fact another Champagné in the parish of Torx about 8 km west of St Jean d'Angely, and this is the place of which Josias was Seigneur. He also owned land at Lisleau (which is probably the modern Liron) and Agère which were "low-lying, enclosed and drained by deep and wide ditches". Agère and Liron are in the area that still fits that description in the triangle formed by the roads linking La Rochelle with Rochefort and Sugeres. Marie owned land at Bernerè and Ponthois and certain property rights in St Savinien (these included ownership of the village bread oven). The estate at Bernerè, 4 km north of St Savien, included a manor house with dovecot, gardens, vineyards and a wine press, to which she and Josias moved from his home after their marriage, and from which she fled.

At about the same time as Josias and Marie de Champagné were lodging in The Hague members of the von Rhenen family were at Memel in East Prussia. Jacobus von Rhenen, or van Rhenen, was born there towards the end of the 17th century. He arrived in Cape Town in 1721 or 1722 and he married Johanna Sickerman in 1725. She died before him and he married for the second time in 1757 Maria Elizabeth Louw. He died in 1764. Except for dates of marriages, births and deaths we know almost nothing about the van Rhenens. The second son of Jacobus, Daniel van Rhenen, was born in 1730 and married Catharina Christina Beck whose father had been born at Kangen, Salz. Daniel's only son, Jacobus, (he had four daughters) who was born in 1762 became a Brigadier General and married Johanna Adriana Bogaardt, the daughter of the Dutch Governor in Chinsara, Bengal. They had thirteen children, and one of them, Frances Barbara, who was born in 1800 was to marry Christopher Godby C.B., an A.D.C to Queen Victoria, and was my great- great-grandmother on the Brooke side of the family; but of that more in due time.

I have referred briefly to the death of Jonas Watson of Lampford, Essex in 1663 and the birth of another Jonas who was to become a distinguished soldier. It is recorded that the younger Jonas was baptised in that same year 1663; but if family and regimental tradition is correct about his age when he died he must have been born in the previous year. Jonas arrived in this world on the eve of great events. Four years later John Churchill, later Duke of Marlborough, was gazetted as an ensign into the King's Regiment of Foot Guards and thus began his military career. In 1685 the Duke of York became James II and only three years later the Glorious Revolution brought William of Orange to England, primarily as far as he was concerned to add England's weight to his fresh coalition against France, the League of Augsburg. When Marlborough took over as Commander-in-Chief for the first time in 1702 he found himself involved in a war of the fortresses. He had to set about clearing the line of the river Maas fortress by fortress. It was not a bad time for a future Chief Bombadier of England to be learning his trade as a soldier.

It is thought that Jonas had probably joined the Artillery at the age of 17 in 1679, and we know that in 1693 he was serving as a Captain of the third of the four companies then in Flanders. Prior to the formation of the Royal Artillery in 1716 the gunner Trains were invariably disbanded after every war.

Thus we find that in 1692 gunners were being withdrawn from the garrisons and castles in England in order to meet a great shortage abroad; but when the Treaty of Ryswick was signed in 1697 the Trains at once were returned from Holland to England, and by the beginning of 1699 Jonas Watson was on half-pay. It was not to be for long, however, because by April 1702 he was back in Holland as a Major of Artillery; and it is believed that he was probably engaged in most of Marlborough's sieges.

In 1704 Marlborough began his march to the Danube, one of the decisive marches of history. It is almost certain that Watson took part in the Battle of Blenheim, fought and won in August of that year, and later in the same decade in the great victories of Ramillies, Oudenarde and Malplaquet, in the last two as a Lieut.-Colonel. In 1709 he was made Chief Bombadier of England, an office instituted by James II in 1686. In 1716 "The cost, drudgery and loss of time entailed by the endless embodiments and disbandments of trains became at length so intolerable, that the permanent Regiment (of Artillery) was formed, established by George I in 1716". At that time Jonas was on half-pay and Borgard, who was to be the first Colonel of the Regiment was busily employed as Chief Firemaster of England. Marlborough died in 1722; and it was not until 1727 that Jonas Watson became the first Lieut.-Colonel of the Royal Artillery and Bogard its first Colonel. At the same time as his appointment as Lieut.-Colonel, Jonas was appointed to command the Artillery in Gibraltar and was present during the second half of the siege of Gibraltar by the Spaniards that took place that year. He was already 64 years old; but his military career was not finished. He was killed at Carthagena in 1740 in his seventy eighth year.

The port of Carthagena on the Caribbean in what is, to-day, north west Columbia withstood a British siege of three months concluded in 1741 during the so called 'war of Jenkins' ear'. The peace policy of Sir Robert Walpole had been brought to an end by a great movement of opinion in favour of a maritime war with Spain. Popular passion was aroused by the old claim of the English, dating from Hawkins and Drake, to trade freely with South America, and by the attempt by Spain to limit that trade. Trevelyan comments that the operations were ill conducted and left the question of South American trade very much where it had been before. Despite its daunting outer forts and encircling walls, Carthagena had been successfully attacked by Drake in 1586 and by the French in 1697. However, on this occasion the British under Sir Francis Vernon failed even though they had a force of 27,000 men and 3000 pieces of artillery. It was defended by the one-eyed, one-armed and one-legged hero, Blas de Lezo, whose statue stands to-day at the entrance of the San Felipe fortress.

Apparently in 1740 Jonas Watson, despite his age, was in command at Woolwich and was ordered to send in the name of the best Artillery Officer he knew, to take command of the Artillery being sent to the West Indies. According to a regimental tradition he obeyed the order in this fashion:--

> "I have the honour to report that the best Artillery officer I know is
> Your most obedient, humble servant,
> Jonas Watson, Lieut.-Colonel."

He was duly appointed and sailed to Carthagena. His son Justly, who also had a distinguished career in the Royal Engineers, sailed with him. Jonas was killed by a round shot during the attack on Fort St. Lazar on the 26th May 1741. A witness reported that the shot which killed him glanced from a tree at some distance from the Battery. Jonas made his last will in July 1740 just before his departure for the West Indies. I have a copy of it. His son Justly, who had served with him as a cadet in Gibraltar and who went with him on this last adventure, was left his library of books and all his maps and instruments "relating to the affairs of Artillery". He made financial provision for his other son, Lovegood, who was Ann's forebear, and, apart from other small dispositions the balance of his possessions went to his wife Miriam, with the request that the household furniture, plate, linen and jewels be divided equally between the sons on her death. A portrait of Jonas Watson, a copy by Alice Grant of an original by an unknown artist, hangs in the Royal Artillery Mess in the bar.

CHAPTER 7. THE 18TH CENTURY.

We have now moved well into the 18th century and by its end almost all the principal tributaries will have emerged and be flowing strongly with their courses clearly defined. It is time to pause and see where all these varied streams are taking us. The Edwards branch will appear for the first time towards the end of the century and will merge later with the two Welsh rivers that we have traced back to medieval times, Thomas and Prichard. The van Rhenens in South Africa will merge with Godbys and then join the Brookes in Yorkshire; they will in their turn meet a stream formed by the merging of two others, Wallich and Collings. All those are my forebears. On Ankaret's side of the family are the Healings; they will merge with those Watsons and Colcloughs whose history we have already traced and various other late joining tributaries, including that of Gillum-Webb. The L'Estranges will meet de Champagnés and with other Irish tributaries, and will then link with McLeans from Islay.

The next hero of our story (in the true sense of the word) is Lt. Colonel Jonas Watson, the grandson of the Chief Bombardier. He married Harriet Colclough. They had eight children. The eldest child Ann, left a vivid account of the Irish rebellion of 1798 and her father's death, which will follow. Her brother Col. Thomas Colclough Watson, who died of cholera, married Sally James. Sally's father, Thomas James, came from a French Huguenot family called Jacques, which like the de Champagnés had settled in Ireland. He married a lady called Wallace (Christian name unknown) who gave Sally the magnificent Dublin made coffee pot, with chinoiserie decoration and a coat of arms, which we use in the family to this day. Sally's granddaughter, Florence Gillum-Webb (whose portrait is at Pont Esgob Mill) wrote a note which records a family legend that the Royal Arms of Scotland on the pot show the descent from "William Wallace who married a daughter of Robert the Bruce". However, she sensibly observes "but it seems that Robert the Bruce had no daughters---The quartering of the Royal Arms with the family arms is at least curious". Florence's caution was well justified as the tale is clearly a myth. The family could conceivably descend from a branch of the William Wallace family (he was executed in 1305); but he certainly did not marry a daughter of Robert the Bruce (or, as far as I can ascertain, any of the five earlier Robert de Bruces). Robert the Bruce, the victor of Bannockburn, (who actually fought for Edward I against William Wallace in 1296) did have a daughter, indeed he had three. Marjorie by his first wife, Lady Isobel of Mar, married Walter the Hereditary Steward of Scotland, whose son Robert II was the first of the Stuart line. There were two daughters by his second wife, Elizabeth de Burgh: Matilda who married Thomas Ysaak, and Margaret who married William, Earl of Sunderland. It is a good legend but a better coffee pot!

Colonel Jonas Watson had served for thirty six years in the 65th & 13th Regiments of foot, and displayed so much skill and enterprise at the Battle of Bunker's Hill and various other engagements in America and the West Indies that he was appointed Governor of the important Fort of Niagara. The story of what happened at Wexford in 1798 was recorded by Florence Gillum-Webb, Ankaret's great-grandmother. She prepared copies of some letters from Jonas to his wife Harriet and the following history of the rebellion. The Ann referred to in the following account was the daughter of Colonel Watson, and Harriet was Ann's daughter.

"The year 1795 was that of the return of my great-grandparents from Canada, and I will now add a few pages--unfortunately only a few which my cousin Harriet wrote years ago partly at her mother's (the Ann of the proceeding pages) *dictation giving an account of what followed*

"In the year 1795 my Father came home from Canada, he sold his commission and retired from the service. He then purchased a beautiful house surrounded by cultivated grounds which from the circumstance of the house being built on a rising was called Mount Anna"

(I believe Mount Anna was 4 or 5 miles from Wexford) FW. *"there he settled himself with every prospect of spending many happy years devoted to the improvement of his Tenantry and the education of his Family, the eldest of whom myself--was now about ten, and the youngest a young babe. Three happy years were spent at Mount Anna during which time I was sent to school at Wexford where my father used frequently to visit me. How shall I ever forget the joy I used to feel when I was called down from time to time to see my beloved Father--every Saturday I came home to stay until Monday. The last Saturday I well remember. My Father and Mother were dining at Fairy Hill, Major Cavenagh's place, which was about two miles from Mount Anna--accordingly I was sent there instead of home.*

On our return that night some of us were walking others driving, we came to a place called the Crosses or Crosses a beg, from which many roads proceeded this being the origin of the name. Near this spot was an Inn from which loud harsh rebellious sounds proceeded: my Father, giving me into the care of one of his friends immediately entered the public house, and after firmly but gently speaking to a very large mob whom he found there collected, he desired them immediately to disperse. In silence he was obeyed, every man returned immediately to his own home.

The next morning as I was walking from room to room with that light and joyous feeling which children can scarcely fail to possess who under like circumstances with myself are feeling the sweets of liberty and freedom of home after the restraints of six days spent at school--as I was thus walking about looking out of the windows, my attention was suddenly attracted by the sight of two horsemen, galloping up the Avenue at the full speed of their horses--I flew down to tell my Father and Mother, and very shortly after they reached the door--My Father went to speak to them, and presently returning said to my Mother "My dearest Harriet the whole county is up in arms and I am sent for to head the Troops. All I have to say to you is--Go as quick as you can to Wexford with the children" Almost immediately after, my Father was gone. What a change had now taken place in my feelings! The calm joy I had felt moments before was now exchanged for horror, alarm, as if some calamity would befall us before night--bustle, hurry, confusion.

With the greatest haste our clothes and other necessaries were packed up, with some hams and other salt meat, and two jaunting cars were laden with them. We then set forth, my mother, my aunt Florence Colclough, my six brothers and sister and a faithful nurse named Ally Parrel. At that time I remember her a tall commanding looking person, her love for my mother and her children was only equalled by her zeal for the Roman Catholic Religion. She was with my mother when I was born, and from that hour to that of her death, she never left our family. Faithful Ally I look back with wonder and think how could we have lived the next few weeks if she had forsaken us. But to continue. Thus with our two jaunting cars laden with ourselves and packages of all kinds we proceeded to Wexford, as fast as our horses could convey us, fearing at every turn in the road that we should be stopped by the Rebels. It was awful as we went on & observed far and near, houses, farms, churches, burning and blazing up to the sky! At last we reached Wexford, and were then safely lodged in the house of my mother's aunt Lady Colclough. The town was in a state of utmost confusion--persons were hastily passing one another with fear and anxiety on their countenances, soldiers were seen in small parties talking to one another, but not one Rebel, at least not one declared Rebel, was to be seen though the back streets were filled with them, only waiting for the appearance of their leaders to join them in the Field.

Such was the state of Wexford during the whole of Sunday. In the evening my Father returned home, he had been endeavouring to keep back the Rebels from Wexford, but was rather hindered in his attempts than otherwise by the thoughtless, rash conduct of one of his officers who insisted on taking his Regiment down into a valley, and of course the Rebels being on the opposite hill, had a very decided advantage over him. My beloved Father was rather low-spirited but my Mother prevailed on him to eat something, which he did. After this we were sent

to bed, and I remember the extreme reluctance I had to leave my Father. Again &
again I returned from the door to throw my arms round him and to bid him good
night, surely I must have had some presentiment of a coming evil.

Early next morning my Mother was awoke by a voice near the bedside-- She
listened. It was the voice of my Father who was earnestly praying-- my Mother
drew aside the curtains & saw the tears were running down the noble, manly face
of her brave husband-- she anxiously enquired the cause of his tears and whether
he was unhappy. He said "No dear Harriet, not at all unhappy, but lie down
again and sleep, for it is too early for you to be awake" He then most tenderly
kissed her and said "Don't make yourself unhappy my love. I trust that if it shall
please God we shall meet again very soon".

He then left the room. Some hours after, my Mother arose, and awaited, with
the greatest apprehension and fears for my Father's return. At last she took me out
with her, and we walked up and down the streets, waiting for some one who could
give us some information about my Father. At last we saw a soldier riding quickly
up the street and as he advanced my Mother cried out "What news of Colonel
Watson?"

"Shot in the heart" was the reply, and the man flew by. My Mother stirred
not, spoke not, but her look was more terrible to me than if she had given way to
a frenzy of griefs. At that moment Colonel de Hunt who had seen the whole came
up to us, and took my Mother into his house, but no effort of her friends could
restore her to any state of feeling beyond the morbid insensibility into which she
had fallen. After doing many things for her she was taken back to Lady Colclough's
and was set in a chair-----"

Here my cousin Harriet's manuscript ends.

Some facts subsequent to what she tells I have known since childhood, and
will presently add; but first I wish to copy a passage taken from Mr Gregor's
History of the French (sic) Revolution.

"The death of Colonel Watson at this critical juncture was a most unfortunate
event for the cause of the loyalists in the County of Wexford, as his long experience,
bravery and military talents would have proved a valuable acquisition to the
subsequent operations.----- A short time previous to the melancholy period of
which we are treating he settled with his Family near Wexford, and as soon as
the insurrection broke out he joined the King's Troops as a volunteer. The advice
which he gave was upon every occasion attended to with that respect due to his
talents and long experience; while the judicious disposition which he made of the
Troops, together with the various works erected for the defence of the Town, again
revived that confidence which had been shaken by the recent disastrous events--
on the melancholy occasion by which the country was deprived of the services of
this gallant officer, Colonel Watson nobly upheld his former character, for when
his cavalry were compelled to retreat by the determined fire of the enemy he--like

Colonel Gardiner at Preston Pans continued to advance at the head of his small party of Infantry till a musket ball brought him from his horse, and the fall of their gallant leader occasioned the rout of the detachment."

And now I must to give some account of what happened to my great Grandmother and her children at that melancholy time. She was as if turned to stone-and in all the alarm and confusion of that terrible day, nothing had power to rouse her till at last Ally, the faithful nurse, said to her

"Mrs Watson. Do you wish the children to be butchered before your eyes."

Thus urged the poor bereaved Mother allowed herself to be conveyed with her children to a small sailing vessel bound for Wales. I suppose here they believed themselves to be in comparative safety- however it seems the Captain was on the side of the Rebels, for when their forces took possession of the Town, he having not yet sailed, would not put to sea, but insisted on landing his unfortunate passengers upon the Quay of the now rebel Town. "Who are these" was asked in no gentle voices, as under the guidance of Ally they endeavoured to make their way back through the rebel crowds to the house that had sheltered them hitherto.

"Colonel Watson's widow and children" firmly answered their intrepid Guardian, and they were not only allowed to pass on unmolested, but I think were favoured in their return, and that a rebel sentry was placed for their protection before the House--such was the name of my great-grandfather respected. There was most inveterate ill will shown however in the case of a Protestant steward of Lady Colclough's. This man was searched for by the rebels with such blood-thirsty determination that a mattress was pierced by their pikes in case he had hidden himself in it. He escaped by hiding himself in a little Theatre that there was in the top of the house.

A cousin of my great-grand mother's was one of the band of young Patriots as they supposed--who had thought to benefit Ireland by preaching to them about Freedom--young men who had caught their ideas from France. This gentleman, one of the Colcloughs, said to my great-grandmother "Ah Harriet! I did not know when this began how it would end!" He lost his life as one of the ring-leaders of the rebellion.

During the period that Wexford was in the hands of the rebels a sort of rude order was maintained, and provisions were served out, trade in the ordinary way being suspended. Ally used to go to the place where meat was to be had, to get what she could for the family, and would come home with the joint whatever it might be and with the indignant exclamation"I could have thrown it at his head! I believe it was a bit of one of Colonel Watson's own sheep."

And the faithful woman in that time of distress used to undo the quiltings of her petticoat and take from that safe receptacle the guineas she had received as wages in time past from her kind master, and devote them now to the service of his widow and children. I believe after a few weeks order was restored, but my great-

grandmother and her family continued to live in Wexford. A sad visit was paid once to Mount Anna, where all that had made it so sweet and charming a house was gone--laid in the grave of the dear Father and Master, or wrecked or made away with. My cousin was about 12 or 13 when she lost her Father; I believe as the years passed by some cheerfulness was restored, and her sweet happy nature re-asserted itself--no doubt the effort to cheer her Mother was of the greatest benefit to herself--and six years after her Father's death, when Captain Hawtrey of the 23rd Regiment came with the recruiting party to Wexford she was acknowledged to be the fairest of all the fair ones there."

She married Captain Hawtrey on the 21st March 1804 in Castlebridge church, County Wexford, just under the monument to Colonel Watson. Jonas Watson lost his life in an attack on the rebel camp at Three Rocks which was on high ground three miles due west of Wexford town. Charles Dickson, in his detailed account of the Wexford Rising, tells us that the position had been chosen with excellent judgement; but his account of Jonas Watson's death differs from that evidently given in Gregor's History, putting him with the cavalry and not at the head of a party of infantry. The camp at the junction of five roads was well suited for ease of assembly from any direction, for observation from the peaks in the vicinity and for rapid movement either in attack or defence. While the insurgents were establishing themselves there after their victory on the 28th May at the battle of Enniscorthy, plans were being made by General Fawcett, in charge of the government forces, to reinforce the garrison in Wexford town. He arrived at Taghmon on the night of the 29th and decided to stop there until the next day. A party of eighty-eight men of the Wexford Militia accompanied by a half battery of gunners with two howitzers passed through Taghmon, apparently unaware that General Fawcett was there and four miles further along the road to Wexford met with disaster in the early morning of the 30th when overwhelmed by rebels pouring down the hill. The garrison of Wexford, expecting the arrival of General Fawcett and alarmed by the appearance of large numbers of people at the Ferrybank end of the bridge into the town decided to attack the camp from the east.

The garrison's force was commanded by Colonel Maxwell who had arrived in the town the previous morning with two hundred men of the Donegal militia and encamped on Windmill Hill. The infantry was supported by five detachments of yeoman cavalry. Charles Dickson states that the cavalry "were accompanied by a retired officer named Lieutenant-Colonel Jonas Watson who served as a volunteer with the rank of sergeant in the Shelmalier Cavalry. They halted on the road opposite Belmont House and Colonel Watson rode forward to reconnoitre the insurgent position. I think he probably turned up the hill road which branches off to the camp about a half-a-mile beyond Belmont. Here he was shot from an insurgent outpost and the whole garrison force, in the absence of any news of the expected reinforcement from General Fawcett, retreated behind the defences of the town".

Jonas Watson was buried in Carrick churchyard. The inscription on his tombstone reads:

> Liutenant Colonel Jonas Watson
> Had been actively employed for thirty years in the service of
> His Country. During which period of his life had often been
> Preserved amidst the shock of Battle
> But it pleased the Almighty that He alone should fall whilst
> Gallantly leading the Yeomanry of this County to attack
> The Rebel force which was posted on the Three Rocks on the
> 30th day of May, 1798
> The consequence of His fall was the immediate evacuation of
> Wexford by the Loyalists

The cousin mentioned in the account was John Henry Colclough (1769-1798). The DNB tells us that he was descended from the family settled in Wexford in the time of Edward III. On the occupation of the Town by the Royalists he fled (with others) to the Saltee Islands and hid in a cave. He was tried by court-martial and executed on Wexford Bridge on 28th June 1798.

By a quirk of fate two of our rivers came close together at Wexford in 1798. We left the L'Estranges in the mid 18th century with 'Handsome Harry' at Moystown in the Kings County. Henry's grandson, Colonel Henry Peisley L'Estrange, who was born in 1776 and died in 1824, married Grace Burdett and was the father of Sir George Burdett L'Estrange and nine other children. Henry Peisley played a more controversial role than Colonel Watson during the Wexford Rising. I will start with the account written by his son George which I have in the form of a manuscript:

" Shortly after my birth the Irish Rebellion broke forth with all its horrors-- my father was then a young man of about 30 years of age, a remarkably handsome well proportioned man of six feet, the Colonelcy of the Kings County Militia having come vacant in consequence of the resignation of Sir Lawrence Parsons whose politics do not appear to have been in unison with the then government. He was afterwards Earl of Hope & the father of the present most highly distinguished and eminently scientific Earl. I do not know whether Sir L. Parsons entertained any unpleasant feeling of jealousy towards my father in consequence of his succeeding him in the command of the Regiment but there did not appear to me to exist between them the same cordiality as I suppose there must have been previously as I see by the Family Bible that he was my Godfather. My father was selected by the

government of the day as the most proper person to succeed and was accordingly appointed Colonel of The Royal King's County Regiment of Militia and Custor Rotulorum of the County, a highly flattering mark of the esteem he was held in at the time when the government must have been well aware that a most critical period was before them and which shortly after burst forth with that violence that shook the constitution of the country to its foundations. Lord Rossmore was at this period Lt Col of the Regiment. I conclude that he was not well pleased at my father being placed over his head, and from what I recollect of him I should think that he had a strong bias towards the liberal or rather more properly speaking at that time the disaffected party. Having made some remarks favourable or not I know not in the presence of my Uncle Christopher who was then Major of the Regiment- the latter remarked " that may be all very well but you would have been glad to see a pike thr' his back". This produced a hostile meeting and they exchanged shots. Lord Rossmore shortly after resigned his commission---My father appointed Herbert Rawson Stepney of Durrow (now called Durrow Abbey) near Lullamore, to succeed him in the Lt Colonelcy, an active and very intelligent magistrate of the County of whom more hereafter. Lord Rossmore was the father of the late peer, a very old friend of mine and also to the Hon H Westonra who was my comrade and intimate companion afterwards in the Scots Fusilier Guards --------------
--------------. The part my father had to act was therefore not an unimportant one, the loyalty of the Regiment he commanded was more than doubtful, and the soldiers deserted to the rebels sometimes in sections with their arms, clothing ,etc. My father, however appears to have been equal to the situation; the Regt- was ordered to Dublin & quartered there during the commencement of the Rebellion. It is not my intention to enter into detail of the Irish rebellion that is already a matter of history, with all its horrors, bloodshed & devastation which marked that cruel and melancholy period of Irish history, but there are some facts relating to it which will come fairly into this family record---the first I shall allude to is that remarkable transaction in which a Captain in the Kings County Militia took a prominent part. I allude to the melancholy fate of the unfortunate misguided and betrayed Sheares---Captain Armstrong otherwise known by the name of "witness Armstrong" had a residence in the neighbourhood of Ballecumber in the Kings County. He, unfortunately for them, became acquainted with the family of the Sheares and was very intimate with them, dining and visiting at their house & entering into all their family details, & thus became in a certain degree mixed up with the United Irishmen of whom it is unnecessary for me to give any detail- -matters however became so serious and he became so mixed up with them, that he became alarmed for his own safety and resolved to disclose the whole plot to his Colonel, my father. The Regiment I have before said were quartered in Dublin which was almost in a state of siege, as there were hordes of rebels in the surrounding country, particularly in the mountains within a few miles if the city. He disclosed

to him that the rebels had prepared a plan to surprise the castle of Dublin at night, which was then defenceless at night, burn the Castle and all the records of the Country and take the Lord Lieutenant prisoner as a hostage up to the mountains, There is little doubt that if this plot had been attempted it would have succeeded and have given a very different and perhaps fatal turn to the civil war that was raging. My father lost no time in communicating this alarming intelligence to the Government who were greatly astounded and nearly paralysed. He was desired to get as much information as possible from witness Armstrong and the Shears were arrested on his evidence though they were not aware of this fact. When in prison they were visited by Armstrong who seemed to condole with them in their alarming position. They assured him that there was but one written Document that they dreaded and that it was locked up in a certain desk in their house, with which he was so well acquainted---they delivered him the key requesting him to go at once and destroy it, but he received it for a far different purpose. He delivered it up to the authorities and hanged the unfortunate and betrayed Sheares, with whose family, whose wives and whose sisters he had been so intimate--and whose children he had so lately dangled on his knee. A case of such unheard of villainy has scarcely been recorded, and when after some period the Regt being stationed in Tarbert and Lt. Colonel Stepney, my respected and well remembered Father in Law, being in command, Captain Armstrong presented himself to join the Regiment again, a meeting of the officers was called and Colonel Stepney being of course the spokesman to convey to him the resolution of the Regiment not to receive him. He, a very talented and highly educated man, was so overcome by his feelings of disgust that he could only say "you are the d--est rascal that ever drew the breath of life" He of course disappeared and enjoyed for many years, for all I know at the present time, the pension of either 5 or £700 a year from the government for useful but degrading information he had given to them. When my father communicated the plans of the rebels to the Lord Lieutenant, I forget whether it was Lord Camden or Lord Cornwallis, the Lord Lieutenant shed tears when convinced of the danger the country and himself individually had escaped, and they offered my father a Baronetcy which however he thought it proper respectfully to decline.

From Dublin the Regiment removed to Loughluistown Camp and shortly afterwards took a part in the battle of Vinegarhill, they afterwards occupied Newtownbarry where there were two small field pieces attached to it. Early one morning the rebels appeared in immense numbers in the surrounding hills, my fathers Regiment now reduced by service and desertion to a small force were in rather a critical position, the town of Newtownbarry being situated in a valley surrounded by hills was scarcely a tenable position. My father therefore thought it prudent to retire with his guns up the road leading up a hill out of the town. The rebels supposing that they were retreating and headed as I have heard by several priests in their canonicals who assured the rebels that they could catch bullets in their hands, rushed into the town, and commenced an indiscriminate scene of plunder and drunkenness, but the small force no sooner reached the summit of the hill, than they faced about threw a few shot and volley amongst the undisciplined rabble, who took to immediate flight and were shot down in their retreat in great numbers. This action I believe obtained my father a good deal of credit, and tho' I have scarcely any recollection of his speaking much about it in after life I attribute it to his very sensitive mind and humane nature, which I have no doubt revolted against such a slaughter of his unfortunate and misguided countrymen and which I know he lamented to the latest period of his life. My mother however frequently described to me awful scenes and hair breadth escapes which occurred in these disjointed times".

The account given by Charles Dickson in his book *The Wexford Rising in 1798*, provides a less creditable explanation than a sensitive mind and humane nature for Henry Peisley L'Estrange's silence. Taking his material from the loyalist historian George Taylor who lived close to Wexford, he states that the garrison under the command of Colonel Henry Peisley L'Estrange of the King's County Militia consisted of some four hundred men, including militia and yeoman infantry, with a number of volunteers and detachments of the 4th Dragoons and the Newtownbarry and Carlow yeoman cavalry. There were also two battalion guns.

"About mid-day the insurgents approached on both sides of the river from the direction of Ballycarney. They brought with them 'a brass six pounder, a howitzer and some ship swivels'. Taking up a position on high ground above the slate quarry, they fired a few rounds and immediately afterwards rushed into the town. Colonel L'Estrange, fearing encirclement, hastily withdrew his infantry without offering any serious resistance and retreated, screened by the cavalry, for a distance of at least a mile up the Carlow road".

Taylor's account continues as follows;

"The rebels entering the town, set the suburbs on fire, plundered the army's baggage, burst open the cellars and drank the spirits in such abundance that becoming intoxicated they ranged thro' the town, shouting and hallooing without any order. This confusion was much increased by the loyalists firing from several of the houses against which they soon bent all their fury. The yeomen...entreated Colonel L'Estrange to return and attack them with his cannon, alleging that as they were quite intoxicated, void of any order and not expecting danger, they would soon be overpowered.

A well timed counter-attack headed by Lieutenant-Colonel Westenra, a volunteer officer named Major Marley and Captain Kerr and proceeded by a few rounds from the two guns which raked the main street and square, drove the insurgents from the town with considerable loss----------

Colonel L'Estrange was regarded by his brother officers as having been guilty of pusillanimous conduct in abandoning the town without a fight and he gave added offence by taking the credit for organising the counter attack to himself and to the volunteer Major Marley, whereas in fact the officer chiefly responsible was Lieutenant-Colonel Westenra (afterwards Lord Rossmore) and he was given no credit. This together with later charges of nepotism in the appointment of officers to his regiment appear to have made Colonel L'Estrange unpopular and eventually the various grievances became the subject of a Court of Enquiry held at Limerick in August-September, 1801. The result was a mild remonstrance and a direction that in future he was to pursue a more equitable system of promotion.

One question and answer during this enquiry are, however, of historical interest. It will be recalled that the infamous Captain J.W. Armstrong, the informer, was an officer in the King's County Militia. Referring to that officer a witness, Lieutenant Thomas Warburton was asked; 'Don't you believe he was directed by Colonel L'Estrange in the most important transaction of his life?' The reply was; 'If he means the prosecution of the Sheares, I believe he acted with the approbation of Colonel L'Estrange'."

A recent student of the 1798 Rebellion, Richard Aylmer, who has read the entire transcript of the Court of Enquiry of 1801, reached the firm conclusion that Colonel L'Estrange and the other officers were being used as pawns in a very large political game. If that is so, and with no other evidence, it would be wrong to wrongly criticise someone who was faced with difficult decisions in a period of confusion and danger.

It is time to introduce two other families that have not previously appeared: Marmaduke Collings of Hull who died in 1785 married Susan, the daughter of Toby Sill of Wakefield. She died in 1816. They had nine children, many of whom, like so many others in that period, served a Britain which was finding its place as an imperial power. Leonard, our ancestor and the eldest, went to India in 1772 and died there in 1797. Marmaduke died in Patua; William went to China; James to America, and Joseph was a Captain in the 12th Regiment. One of them must have been the Captain Collings, Charge d'affaires to the Portuguese Court, who is the subject of the portrait which was sold at Christies on 7th May 1943, attributed to Gainsborough, and which was bought by my father. It now hangs in our London home. In the same sale there was a portrait of John Smith of Welton in Yorkshire which was the same size but attributed to Reynolds. It seems likely that they came from the same owner. As Leonard's daughter Mary married a John Smith and his father, also called John, came from Welton, I believe that Leonard must be the subject of our portrait, and presumably he was in Portugal before his departure for India. Sophie Collings married Dr Nathaniel Wallich, a widowed Dane, who is my great-great -grandfather. Nathaniel Wallich was born in 1786 in Copenhagen, the son of Lazarus Wallich Wulff, a wealthy Jewish merchant from Germany. Having graduated M.D. in his native city, he entered the Danish medical service when still very young, and in 1807 was surgeon to the Danish settlement at Serampore. A world famous botanist, we shall hear more about him as his career develops in the 19th century.

The first Healing, John, about whom we know anything had appeared, as we have seen, towards the end of the 17th century. All his seven children were born in the same century. The eldest son, William was baptised in 1675 and died in 1711. His younger brother, John, was born at Deerhurst in 1686 and died in 1729. Like his father before him his will was proved in Gloucester. We then have four consecutive Samuels, the first born in 1713 and the last in 1799 at Tewkesbury. It was under the leadership of this last Samuel who died in 1883 that the family would develop the flower mill that was to dominate Tewkesbury business and the river skyline, though fortunately without threatening the overall dominance of Tewkesbury Abbey.

In Yorkshire the other family mill prospered. The four generations that succeeded John Brooke who had founded the woollen business in the reign of Henry VIII continued to lease New Mill; but in the middle of the 17th century William Brooke bought it, and with it the water rights that were so vital for the business. William's initials can still be seen on an old water trough at Greenhill Bank. He died in 1683. The second William in the business (1704-1770) married Sarah Kaye of Woodsome in the Colne valley, who brought with her a useful dowry. Together they built Exchange House in the village of Holme where their initials are carved on a stone above the front door. Helped by Sarah's resources, William rented a new mill in a part of the valley where there was more water. Two of his notebooks survive, part of an astonishing and invaluable set of business records that constitutes a comprehensive history of the firm from the 17th century down to the start of the next millennium. William's son, John, formed John Brooke and Son in 1785; but it was during the time of his grandson, another William (1763-1846) that the whole scale of the business changed. Once again marriage to a wealthy heiress proved invaluable. William's marriage to Hannah Clapham brought a dowry of £10,000 which enabled him to buy Armitage Bridge Mill in 1798. Here was more land and more water to power the wheels and later a massive turbine. This William represented the tenth generation since the foundation of the business in 1541. He bought one of James Watt's new steam engines, manufactured black and blue cloth, the latter for sale to the Navy. Its production involved the purchase of expensive indigo dye, the largest item of expense at the time. It was a well justified expenditure because the firm always did well when the country was at war, and the Napoleonic wars meant that this was a prosperous period. In 1809 the firm made a profit of

£8000 on a turnover of £49,000, substantial sums in the money values of the time. William became involved in banking and the new railway companies, and his reputation was such that he was offered £50,000 funding without security. He built Northgate House, Northgate Mount and Armitage Bridge House, and lived himself at Northgate Mount. He retired in 1825 and died in 1836.

In Wales, as I recorded in an earlier chapter, William Prichard had sold Goytre Manor in about 1730 to Charles Hanbury Williams and had gone to live at The Hill, Trostrey, near Llanover. He died in 1755. His son, who was also called William, was baptised at Goytre in 1718 and died in Chepstow in 1795. Two Thomas Prichards, one born in 1765 in Bristol, and his son in 1791, take us to the end of the century.

We had left the Thomas family in Coychurch during the middle of the 17th century. The lives of the children of Edward Thomas who died in 1645 were all disrupted by a duel fought by the second son, Edward, who fled to Ireland and changed his name to Rowland Thomas. He killed Edmund Thomas of Coyty with a rapier on 4th February 1661. His younger brother the Reverend David Thomas, Rector of Coyty was tried on account of the duel and acquitted in Glamorgan. He was re-indicted and at length discharged before the King's Bench in Hereford. Another brother, John Thomas, a surgeon, went to Portugal on account of the duel and died on his passage home on 1693. Robert Thomas, the eldest son, a doctor, also fled on account of the duel to Leyden and sold the Tregrose Estate, but later returned to Wales. His eldest son, Edward a surgeon, born in 1665, bought back the Tregrose Estate and, more significantly, married Anne Morgan, the heiress of Pwllywrach. They had seventeen children, fourteen of whom Edward saw brought up and provided for. Through those seventeen there is almost an infinity of connections with other Glamorgan families.

David Thomas, the 17th and youngest child and sixth son, was born on the first Sunday after Michaelmas 1703. He married in 1739 Susanna, the daughter of Francis Coppinger of Lincoln's Inn, the same family of Coppinger whose early history we have already traced. Two of our rivers have joined. The junction is commemorated by a particularly handsome contemporary coffee pot bearing the arms of the two families which for a time was in the possession of my father but which is now owned by my cousin Mathew Prichard and is at Pwllywrach. Edward died in 1769 and Susanna died before him in 1750. Their son David of Pwllywrach was born in London in 1742. He married Mary Curre in 1765, was High Sheriff of Glamorgan in 1777, and died in Bath in 1830. He altered Pwllywrach in 1770.

This is where we can again play the John of Gaunt game! Susanna's great-grandfather was married to a daughter of Lord Burgh of Gainsborough, and her great-great-grandfather, Thomas Coppinger, married Frances Brooke, the daughter of William Brooke (Lord Cobham), and Dorothy Nevill. Dorothy Nevill was both a direct descendent of John of Gaunt by the Beauforts and of his younger brother, Edmund, Duke of York, by way of the Earls of Gloucester, Worcester and Lords of Abergavenny. Her immediate ancestors were among the grandest in the land; in addition to those already referred to, they include Somersets, Kents, Warwicks and Northumberlands, not to speak of Catherine Woodville, the sister of Elizabeth, Queen of Edward IV. Long after those words were written I found among my father's papers (not in his hand)) a dozen or so sheets playing the same game. They set out to show that there were many different lines of descent to my Prichard grandmother, not just from English kings, but from the kings of France, Scotland and Ireland as well, and involving most of the greatest families in the land. The preparation of those genealogies must have consumed much time and effort. As we shall discover in a later chapter, it was a particularly odd exercise to undertake on behalf of the wife of a radical reforming clergyman who spoke at miners' rallies and on Labour and Liberal platforms; but perhaps that is why it was undertaken!

William Thomas, who was born at Pwllywrach in 1770, served first as a private soldier in Dominica and then he had a commission bought for him by his mother in 1791 in the 60th Rifles. He quarrelled with his Commanding Officer and challenged him across the Mess table with pistols. He arrived home at Pwllywrach driving a four in hand with a black servant. He was in debt and asked his sister Lydia to make peace with his parents. It was William's younger brother Robert, the Rector of Itton and Colwinston, who inherited the Pwllywrach estate on the death of his father in 1830. His sister, Mary, induced her brother in 1830 to lease Pwllywrach saying she would look after it for her nephew, David. On the latter's arrival she waved the will triumphantly in his face. Although Robert promised David to re-alter his will he had not done so when he died in 1830. Mary moved to Lansdowne Terrace, Cheltenham where she lived extravagantly, getting through as much as the money as she was able and cutting down large numbers of trees around Colwinston. Mary's nephew and my great-great-grandfather, David, was thus kept out of Pwllywrach for six years and could not marry until 1837. When he was summoned to his Uncle Robert's deathbed from Bristol, he missed the coach which cost him £20,000. It was said that he was never again late for anything.

While these interesting events were happening in Glamorgan, another major river suddenly makes its appearance in Cardigan. It seems likely that forebears of the Edwards family had been farming there perhaps for centuries; but if so their traces have been lost in the boggy uplands of West Wales.

William Edwards of Hafodygofaint makes his appearance in the mid 18th century. 'In the list of the several Freeholders and Leaseholders of the several Hundreds, Precincts and Commons within the County of Cardiganshire' for 1760 appears the name of William Edward of Hafodygofaint. His son, Joseph, was born in 1766 at Rhydyrefail, Llerod in Cardiganshire. He married Catherine Williams of Gwnnws and in 1815 moved to Hafodygofaint, Gwnnws. He died at Hendrefelen in 1855, aged 89. Joseph Edwards is described by George Lerry in his book *Alfred George Edwards, Archbishop of Wales* as "Joseph Edwards of Hendrefelen in the Parish of Ysbythy Ystwyth- -a devout and earnest man much interested in the revival then within the church". He was one of the converts of Daniel Rowlands of Llangeitho, and he accompanied the Reverend Ebenezer Morris, Twrgwn (to whom he was related) through North Wales as a "Cynghorwr" during his itinerant ministry. Hendrefelen was the ancient home of an ancient family of the name of Hughes, more than one of this family were Sheriffs of Cardiganshire. The last of them in the male line, Thomas Hughes, died on 8th May 1790 in his 67th year. The Edwards family either settled at Hendrefelen on the death of Thomas Hughes or (according to Lerry) in 1830 when the family of Hughes left. Joseph and Catherine are commemorated on a tombstone in Gwnnws churchyard.

Up in the island of Islay, Archibald, the great-grandson of Allan McLean of Shuna was born in 1699 and died in 1750. His son, John, lived at Octofad, on the edge of the great inlet, Loch Indaal, that divides the island almost in two. There he married Janet, the daughter of Archibald Campbell of Jura, who was born in 1738 and died in 1773. He was known as "John of the loud voice" and it was said that he could be heard at Laggan almost five miles away across the water to the east. His son, Lachlan of Cladach, married Lucy Campbell, the daughter of James Campbell 5th of Ballinaby. One of their five children, Alexander Colin born in 1796, was a ships captain and ship owner. On his return from a voyage to Java he married in 1828 Margaret McNeill of Ardnacross on the Kintyre peninsular; and settled at Laggan, a substantial property not far from the river of the same name. There is a family legend that while in the Far East he was asked to deliver a bolt of cloth to the McNeill family at Ardnacross; and that it was during that call that he fell in love with Margaret. Perhaps it is true; but Margaret's father, Neil, had been born at Kidalton on Islay and she herself was born on the island, so it seems likely that the two families must have known each other long before he sailed to the Far East. What is certain is that it was the bold involvement in commercial ventures in Java of Alexander Colin and his wife's two brothers, John McNeill 5th of Ardnacross and Alexander McNeill, that changed the fortunes of the family. The story of the involvement of the McLean and McNeill families in the Far East trading company Maclaine Watson is for later chapters (and is set out in full in the Appendix). Both Laggan and Octofad are there to-day and probably look much as they did at the end of the 18th century.

We move out of that century with a number of streams widely differing in character all flowing towards an eventual junction in the sixth decade of the 20th century; but before they get there the world will have changed out of all recognition

CHAPTER 8.   THE 19TH CENTURY.

I pick up the story again with the founding in Batavia in 1827 of Maclaine Watson (by Gillian Maclaine from Mull and Edward Watson from London), and its sister company McNeill & Co (by John McNeill 5th of Ardnacross) in the same year in Samarang. Gillian Maclaine tragically lost his life in a hurricane in 1838. The sons of the ship owner, Alexander Colin McLean, Lachlan (born 1830) and Neil (born 1836), went to Java in the middle of the century and took over the task Gillian and their uncles had started in making Maclaine Watson hugely successful and "second only to the Dutch NHM (*Nederlandsche HandelMaatschappis*) in terms of economic muscle and as suppliers of capital to the sugar industry" in Java. They both returned to Scotland rich men. Lachlan got back to Islay and in 1868 rented Islay House. The plans for the first phase of that house had been laid by Sir Hugh Campbell of Cawdor when he visited his property in 1667. In the early 18th century the Islay property was acquired by Daniel Campbell of Shawfield (Great Daniel). He and his Shawfield heirs did much to modernise agriculture on the island and improve the condition of their impoverished tenants; but by the 1840s the effort was proving too much and in 1848, after 120 years of Shawfield rule, the estate was sequestrated and the property was sold to James Morrison, a London merchant banker and Member of Parliament for the Inverness Boroughs (1840-7). The Morrison family hold it to this day, the Campbell link being restored when the granddaughter of the last Campbell owner married the future Lord Margadale. When Lachlan McLean returned from Java, Islay House was empty, and he rented it from James Morrison together with the shootings. I have inspected the rent books still kept in the estate office at Bridge End which show that the first rent was £60 a year and the initial lease for ten years. The lease was renewed at an annual rent of £200; but in 1880 Lachlan died of appendicitis. He had married Elizabeth, the daughter of the Rev. Alexander Cameron of Kilchoman on the west side of the island. Alexander Cameron had joined the Free Church in 1843 and was Minister until 1872. He was born in 1787 and died in 1872. The living had been presented by George IV in 1824. He married Mary, the daughter of Carter Stiles of Bristol. In addition to Elizabeth there were four other children. The manse stands there to-day unaltered in its sheltered valley below the derelict church; it is a guest house and restaurant. In the churchyard we found the memorial stone to 'Hector McLean of the Two Hearts' who was, I believe, the Maclean given the first name Lachlan who died in the bloody skirmish beside Loch Gruianart described in an earlier chapter.

Elizabeth, the daughter of the manse had never left Islay, but on the death of her husband she immediately took herself and her seven children to London and sent her four daughters to expensive finishing schools. She never returned to the island. The eldest son, Colin, became Chief Constable of Inverness and married Dora Thomson. They were the grandparents of Ann's cousin, Colin Fraser-Mackenzie; his brother Alexander followed the family tradition and went to Java (creating the Alexander McLean Trust from which in due time Ann and the children were to benefit); Neil was engaged to Rosie Springfield, but was killed by a train! Mary (or May) married Percy Howard to begin the line of our Howard cousins (their sons Ken and Charles both worked for the firm); Lucy did not marry; Nora married Harold Woodall and had no children; and Margaret was, as we shall see, to marry Percival L'Estrange. Nora lived for a time in a fine Elizabethan House, Waterstone, in Dorset and we have inherited some of her furniture.

Lachlan's younger brother Neil, a partner in Maclaine Watson from 1871 to 1879, who died in 1923 worth £180,000 (quite a sum in those days), was the grandfather of Callum McLean of Breda, and the forebear of our Macpherson cousins. His sister, Anabella Gillies, married Robert Ballingal to begin another line of cousins who were to contribute to the Maclaine Watson story. Islay House was vastly extended towards the end of the century and Lord Margadale and the Morrisons entertained there on the grand scale; but the house and a few acres, but not the main estate, was sold to an American in 1985. He was the personal pilot to the Saudi Royal Family, and there was speculation that the house was being held as a bolt hole to which they could escape in the event of serious trouble in the kingdom. It has since been placed on the market .

We left the L'Estrange family still in Ireland and Sir George Burdett L'Estrange explaining his father's part in the rebellion of 1798. His book, *The Recollections of Sir George L'Estrange* takes up the tale in his somewhat discursive style. Henry Peisley had ten children and we must leave most of them until at the end we come back to explore the delta and learn what all our numerous cousins were up to. Enough for the moment to say that many of George Burdett's brothers and sisters married well, and their portraits can be found on the walls of Irish country houses, many of which to-day are hotels or have been kept going by becoming up-market B & Bs. George explains how his eldest brother Henry, born in 1793, *'got a commission in the old fighting 5th, and went through the campaigns for three years in Picton's division, taking an honourable part in the numerous bloody battles and sieges, including Badajoz, Ciudad Rodrigo, &c. He was at the side of his gallant colonel, Ridge, entering the citadel of Badajoz, in the front of his regiment, when Ridge received his death-wound, greatly lamented by Lord Wellington and the whole army'.*

George Burdett, born on 1797, was sent to Westminster School in 1807, but left at the age of 16 and received an Ensign's commission initially in the King's County Militia. The story of his departure for the Peninsula in the company of his cousin Edmund, who was to die on the field of Waterloo, is remarkable. In November 1812, while a fleet of transports lay at Spithead, George was presented with a commission without purchase in the 31st Regiment, and was ordered to march a body of Irish volunteers from Portsmouth to Ashford in Kent to undergo preliminary training.

"I must confess they were a set of wild Irishmen, whom I had some trouble and difficulty in coaxing along the march for several days. They were unarmed, but ready notwithstanding for any row that might turn up. My father having given me a good horse, I rode at their head, and hit upon an expedient which I found very successful, which was to play Irish tunes for them on the flute, at which I was no great proficient, but they stepped along cheerily to their native country airs, and I joined with them all in safety at Ashford.".

Soon he took them back to Portsmouth and embarked for Lisbon. During the voyage out his cousin Edmund entertained him with an account of his astonishing escapes from the fortress of Verdun and the dungeons of Bitche. In January 1813 George took temporary command of a small detachment of the Grenadier Guards in order to escort twenty five mules laden with dollars to headquarters. He was still only 16. He then received a sort of roving commission to join the 2nd Division, Sir Rowland Hill's, in winter quarters near Placentia; and eventually he found his Regiment, the 31st. His first experience of battle was at Vittoria, the great allied victory on the field of which the Duke of Wellington obtained so many of the treasures that now occupy Apsley House and Stratfield Saye.

"As we approached the wood, the fire from it slackened, and we entered and passed through without meeting much opposition; but when we emerged at the opposite side, we saw the dark line of the French army, still in their position, within point blank distance. A perfect hailstone of bullets was poured down upon us, which, if it had lasted, must have swept us all into eternity. But we pushed forward, and the French turned. Looking to my right, I saw my captain, Girdlestone, wounded and supported by the bugler. I rushed over to him; he seized me by the hand, gave it a hard squeeze, and said to me, "Go on, my boy! Your name will be mentioned". I felt a certain choking sensation in my throat; a tear swelled into my eye, but it had not time to fall. I ran on frantically to the front, screaming at the top of my voice, "Come on, 31st!" which cry could not have reached the ears of half of my company, in consequence of the roar of the battle. But these brave fellows did not require to be called to advance; the only difficulty

was to keep them back--------By the wound of Girdlestone I found myself placed in command of the light company of the 31st, who had been through the greater part of the Peninsular War, and, though reduced in numbers, were as gallant a lot of men as ever existed. I began to feel that, at the age of sixteen, I was placed in a very responsible position, and determined to keep myself as cool and steady as was possible."

Except for one short period, he held that position for the rest of the war, much of it conducted in the heart of the Pyrenees. After one particularly tense battle when the British and their allies were falling back through the pass of Roncesvalles he watched the 21st Fusiliers charge the French.

" *I asked afterwards who the gallant youths were who carried the colours with such commendable effect, and was informed that one of them was Francis Russell, in whose room I and the second Marquis of Anglesey slept at Westminster; and we were both his fags. " Hoorah for Westminster!" said I".* George was with the army as it drove the French out of the Peninsular and across the Pyrenees, and was present at the final Battle of Toulouse on 10th April, 1814 which ended the war. A few days later he was joined by his uncle Colonel, later General, Guy Carlton L'Estrange who distinguished himself at Albuera and in other engagements in the Peninsular. George Burdett later got a commission in the Guards, served for seven years in London, Windsor, and the Tower and at the end exchanged on half-pay. The rest of his life never quite lived up to those extraordinary years when as a boy of sixteen and seventeen he behaved with such bravery and dash.

In particular, he never really got over the loss of The Moystown estate in 1852 and the failure of his subsequent rather desperate attempts to recover it. It fell victim as so many Irish estates did to poverty and the so called 'confiscation acts'. Apart from the human suffering, one result of famine in Ireland was the ruination of many Irish landlords. One third of landlords received no rents during the famine years and were unable to pay interest on their mortgaged properties. It is estimated that 10 per cent of landlords went bankrupt. In October 1847 an Act was passed which enabled those who had claims against landlords to petition to have an estate sold in the Court of Encumbered Estates. Initially estates were sold at bargain prices and in many cases both creditors and owners of estates were left penniless. During the next thirty years almost five million acres or a quarter of the land in Ireland was dissolved through the Encumbered Estates Act. Ann and I have sat on the foundations of the old house on its site between the Shannon and the Brosna river not very far from Shannon Bridge and shared George Burdett L'Estrange's sense of loss. It was the end of a three hundred year old connection. It would seem from family correspondence that George was often in debt and that he borrowed from relations and friends in a manner that sometimes strained relationships; but equally it is clear that he had many friends and was welcome in Temple House in County Sligo and in many other homes of his widely connected family. A number of letters written in the 1860s and 1870s indicate that relations were meeting obligations that he could not honour; and there is a hint that he may have had to dispose of some of the family portraits. Despite all that he records that he was Chamberlain during the reigns of eight Lord Lieutenants of Ireland, and he was Gentleman Usher of the Black Rod to the Order of St. Patrick from 1858 until his death in 1878. He was knighted by the Earl of Carlisle at Dublin in 1860. By a strange coincidence his granddaughter, Rhoda, was to marry the 10th Earl of Carlisle in 1894. He and his wife, Louisa Vincentia, had fifteen children, adding substantially to the vast circle of cousins; but we need only concern ourselves with his fourth son Paget, Ann's great-grand father.

Paget was born in 1831. He was a Colonel in the Royal Artillery. He served with some distinction in the Crimean War. He was in the trenches with the siege train before Sebastopol, where he was promoted Captain, and at the bombardments of 6th and 17th April, 1855; and on 17th June when he was severely wounded. He was at the Battle of Tchernaya, after which he was mentioned in despatches. After the Crimea he served in India and in 1863 he was in command of a Battery before Lucknow. Because of the state of the accounts of the Battery following the Indian Mutiny he demanded a Court of Enquiry. He claimed that he was often obliged to pay the officers and men out of his own funds. He was promoted Colonel in 1877 and commanded an Artillery District in India in 1881.

He married first in India in 1865, the daughter of General William Henry Ryves of the 8th Cavalry, Bengal Army, but she died in Nova Scotia in December 1868, but not before giving birth to two children, Eudo and Rhoda. He then married Eliza, the widow of Colonel Colin Campbell of the 46th Regiment and the daughter of Francis Gibbes. Eliza is, I fear, a black hole in my tale; and so far I have found no trace of that particular stream. They had two children, Ankaret's grandfather Percival Hastings and Dora. Despite his service in the Crimea and India, Paget missed the promotion to Brigadier General to which he felt he was entitled. This was not just a matter of wounded pride but anxiety about his pension as a Colonel. I have a draw full of his letters, including many that he wrote to his children from the Crimea, from Pembrokeshire, where he was stationed and lived for a good many years, and from India. After his retirement, he bombarded the Commander in Chief, the Duke of Cambridge, and the War Office with petitions; and he wrote to many others in the Service with whom he had served including Field Marshals Roberts and Wolseley. Lord Wolseley in a letter of sympathy to his wife after his death described him as "one of my oldest companions in arms. Many was the day we passed together in the Batteries before Sebastopol". Sadly Paget's representations were all to no avail. Many distinguished soldiers provided testimonials and The Field Marshals replied in kind, indeed in affectionate, terms; but poor Paget did not get his promotion and felt a sense of burning resentment until his death in 1905. However, his obituary notes that he was granted a reward for distinguished and meritorious service in 1889, and this presumably took the form of some financial payment.

His son, Percival Hastings, Ankaret's grandfather, was educated at Sedbergh, where he won the 10 mile Fell Race, and Queen's College Oxford. He was Assistant Master at Malvern College, and the Author of *A Progressive Course of Comparative Geography* which by 1913 had gone to six editions. Curiously little was said about him in the family in his later years, and as a letter from his son Guy (which I quote from below) makes clear he became a very sick man, probably suffering from shell shock as a result of war service. It was he who married Margaret McLean, creating the junction of two of our rivers, and in the happier days of his youth their children, Guy and Betty, were born.

We return to Ireland. Ann, the older sister of Thomas Coleclough Watson who died of cholera, dictated the vivid account of her father's death in the 1798 rebellion. Thomas had nine children and the youngest, Annie Florence, married Major General Edward Atlay. General Atlay's brother was Bishop of Hereford. They were the children of the Reverend Henry Atlay. Florence Atlay, the daughter of Edward and Annie Florence, married Colonel Henry Gillum-Webb of the Worcestershire Regiment. They were Ann's great-grandparents. The fine portrait that hangs in our dining room suggest that we should know much more about them than we do. The note already quoted about the coffee pot and the Wallace connection and the handwritten account of the Irish Rebellion suggests a woman of intelligence who took an interest in the family history. We know even less about the Colonel and his Webb forebears except that it was he who added the Gillum to the name; but we do know that his grandfather "lived in London in great style on the proceeds of a brewery" and that his father who married a lady called Eliza Ann "was a well known man about London Town and a great gambler to boot. He lost most of his money at games of chance and moved to Bedford". Fortunately his sister, Julia Ann Webb, "lived comfortably in Cadogan Gardens" and "left a considerable sum of money to Henry Gillum-Webb and Sophie Webb" (his sister). This Sophie married George Edward Langley, the grandfather of Sir William Kenneth Allen (another cousin) who is the source of information about the Webbs. Florence's daughter, Evelyn Florence, Ann's grandmother, is the subject of the charming portrait painted when she was a child that hangs with her mother's portrait. She was to marry Frederick Henry Healing, the great-grandson of Samuel Healing referred to in the *Tewkesbury Register and Magazine*, as Samuel Healing, Senior, maltster, who was born in 1761. Samuel's wife, Sarah, died in 1842. As two of their sons (the first, William dying as an infant) were given the Christian name Chandler, I wonder if Sarah had belonged to the Chandler family who were also Prominent maltsters in the town. The younger William Chandler Healing died at the age of 29 in 1832, The second son, Samuel, (1791-1883), who previously owned five smaller mills and a brewery, built Healing's steam powered flour mill in Quay Street in 1865. It was to be greatly enlarged in 1889 and again in 1935.

At the time when I married Ann, the local garage in Bredon was run by a Chandler and I had a row with him after he crashed my car returning it to me from the car park at the end of a dance. It seems possible that he was a cousin of the family, and I wonder if my father-in- law had ever considered that possibility. If he did it was one of those topics not talked about in the family!

Described in a local journal in the first decades of the 19th century as a maltster, we see Samuel emerging as a prominent citizen of Tewkesbury. In 1829 we find him contributing to a fund in support of a candidate favourable to Reform who was persuaded to stand in opposition to the two Tory M.P.s for the town, both of whom opposed the Great Reform Bill. In the 1840s he was a Town Councillor, then Alderman and finally Mayor. He married Mary Pitt Kingsbury (about whom I know nothing except that she died in 1862) and died himself in 1883. Two of his sons died quite young, one at the age of 19 and the other 26; one son William J. Healing prospered, became a J.P. and acquired Oldfield, a substantial house just outside Tewkesbury. William's daughter married John Argyll Robertson (and the link to more cousins); while Frederick Henry married Evelyn Gillum-Webb.

Two more of our rivers have merged. Ann's grandfather not only managed the family mill, which we see in the picture at Pont Esgob painted in 1906 as a very substantial building; but was Captain of Tewkesbury Cricket Club at a time when the Healings could field a complete cricket XI. The Tewkesbury Cricket Club was unbeaten in 1908. In that year, while playing a side that included county players and was captained by G. L. Jessop, the great England cricketer, F. H. Healing bowled Jessop in both innings.

Having brought Healings and Gillum-Webbs together, we now return to Wales. David Thomas whom had been kept out of his inheritance for six years by his aunt and had learned a sharp lesson on the importance of punctuality married his Prichard cousin Eliza, the daughter of Thomas Prichard and Susan Horler of Bristol. He died in 1834 three years before the marriage of his daughter. David and Eliza had five children. The eldest daughter, Mary

Anna, in 1858 married her cousin, Charles John Collins Prichard, who was the nephew of her mother, Eliza and the son of Eliza's brother Thomas (born in 1791) and his wife, Judith. Thus in two consecutive generations Prichard and Thomas blood inter-mingled and a new and greater river was formed.

Charles John Collins Prichard was my great-grandfather. He was born in 1830, married in 1858 and died in 1903. His wife, Mary Anna, inherited Pwllywrach from her brother, Hubert de Burgh Thomas, in consideration of the fact that her husband had redeemed many debts and mortgages of Hubert de Burgh who died unmarried in 1878. The family tree notes that she was responsible for the stained glass windows at Pwllywrach, the tiled floor of Colwinston church and "many other vandalisms". There were nine children of the union. Hubert Cecil, born in 1865 was my cousin, Mathew's, grandfather. Edith Lily married the Rev William Alfred Edwards about whom we shall shortly hear more. Evelyn Mary was the grandmother of my cousin, Patrick Carnegie; and Bertie Coppinger Prichard left all his and his first wife's money to a donkeys' home in Ireland!

We now have to trace the story of the descendants of Joseph Edwards of Hendrefelen. He and Catherine had six children. Three of the sons became beneficed clergymen of the church in Wales. Several more clergy are descended from the eldest daughter Ann; and the youngest daughter, Mary, was the mother of clergymen. The eldest son, William, my great-great-grandfather, who was born in 1800 and died in 1868, was Curate of Strata Florida, and then of Llanwyddelan, Montgomeryshire, Rector of Llanymawddwy and Vicar of Llangollen. The DNB entry for William's son, Alfred George, who was to become the first Archbishop of Wales, describes the *Bryn* where he was born as "a small manor house used as the rectory of Llanymawddwy, a remote, wide-spreading, mountain parish in Merionethshire", and describes the family as "typically Welsh in its strongly clerical character. His grandfather was a devout churchman, three of whose four sons became clergymen in Welsh parishes. His home background was austere, but cultivated. His father's income never reached £450 a year". Another son, Edward, who stayed on the farm at Hendrefelen, was a leader in the social and religious life of the district in which he lived. One who knew him said "A better speaker in the Welsh language I never heard, even on the hills where the pith of all eloquence is to be found".

William was ordained direct from Ystrad Meurig Grammar School just down the valley from the family home. This was one of the licensed Grammar Schools in Wales from which young men were ordained without going to any university. When in 1849 William moved to his last parish, Llangollen, he found that the majority of people in the town were Nonconformists; but by the time of his death in 1868 he was greatly loved by all in the parish.

In 1828 he had married Sarah Wood, the daughter of Thomas Wood of Painswick in Gloucestershire, who came from a prosperous and well regarded family. George Borrow on his famous tour of Wales paid several visits to the Llangollen Vicarage in 1854. In *Wild Wales* he records how "*On the appointed evening we went , myself, wife and Henrietta, and took tea with the Vicar and his wife, their sons and daughters, all delightful and amiable beings--the eldest son a fine intelligent young man from Oxford, lately admitted into the Church, and now assisting his father in his sacred office*". The son referred to, Ebenezer Wood, afterwards became Vicar of Ruabon and Canon of St. Asaph. Alfred George, the future Archbishop of Wales was only six years old at the time of this visit. He was to be Bishop of St Asaph for 47 years and the dominant figure defending the interests of the Church in Wales during the great political battles over Tithes and Disestablishment.

The other three sons all became clergy as well. Henry Thomas (educated at Westminster School, where he was a 'Bishops Boy' and holder of the Williams exhibition), probably did more than any other man to bring the Welsh language back into a central place in the work of the Church in Wales and became Dean of Bangor before a tragic death by suicide in 1884; while Bickerton was was a Vicar of two parishes and the father of a popular Rector of Tenby who became the owner of Fynone, a Nash House in north Pembrokeshire. Many years later, as a Conservative candidate in Pembrokeshire, I was to gain a much enhanced reputation from being a relation of the much loved Lizie, widow of Dr William Bickerton Edwards, who owned Fynone. The only daughter of William and Sarah (Borrow was wrong when he mentioned daughters) was to marry James Lewis of Plas Draw near Aberdare, and become the grandmother of Jimmy Windsor Lewis, Welsh Guards, who commanded the Guards Brigade and Joan Curzon Howe-Herrick of a prominent Yorkshire family.

My great-grandfather, William Joseph, was for forty one years Rector of Llandow in Glamorgan, the living to which he had been appointed in 1858 by Jesus College, Oxford where he had been a scholar and Powis Exhibitioner. He was highly regarded as a linguist and coach and several of his classical text books were highly praised. He married Emily de Burgh, daughter of Walter Hussey de Burgh of Donmore House, County Kildare and of Drumleen, County Limerick. She died at the age of 83, having outlived her husband who died in 1899. This is another tributary which I have failed to trace. My grandfather William Alfred Edwards was like his father Welsh speaking. He was educated at Cowbridge Grammar School and Jesus College, Oxford. After graduating at Jesus where he became a Fellow, he was ordained a deacon in 1892 and a priest in 1893. He was curate of Wharton, Cheshire, 1892-3, Vicar of Bunbury with Calveley and Reckforton, Cheshire, 1894-7, and Vicar of St Thomas Hyde, Cheshire, a large industrial parish, 1897-9. His first sermon at St Thomas Hyde on the need for harmony in private and national life was fully reported in local papers, one of which made the comment that the sermon "stamped him as a man of strong personality; (and) as a clergyman who takes a broadminded, progressive view of social as well as religious matters". When in 1899 he became Rector of Llangan in Glamorgan, his progressive views put him in the limelight well beyond the boundaries of the parish and made him a controversial figure in some quarters. One newspaper told its readers that "The rector of Llangan---who figured prominently at a recent demonstration of the Garw and Ogmore miners, holds advanced democratic views, and is becoming highly popular among the working classes of Mid-Glamorgan. The rector is quite an enthusiastic Radical". The speeches that he had made to the miners had been at meetings organised by the South Wales Miners' Federation and the Independent Labour Party. He was in great demand on Labour and Liberal platforms during the 1906 General Election. He was a temperance reformer. After he had been criticised by a fellow clergyman in a letter to the Western Mail for having become actively involved in politics, one commentator wrote "Socialists are generally the most extreme of persons, but the rector of Llangan is a socialist without being extreme. Temperance reformers are the most intemperate of people but the Rector of Llangan is a temperance reformer without being intemperate". Unlike his uncle, the Bishop of St Asaph, he was a supporter of Disestablishment and published a pamphlet about it. He was an eloquent speaker in Welsh and English and won a prize at The National Eisteddfod for a biography of the Liberal statesman, Lord Aberdare.

His obituary in the Western Mail contained the comment "He received all attacks upon him with unfailing good humour, and his geniality won him many devoted friends among his political opponents and those who differed from him on matters of principle". He had defended himself effectively in a letter to that paper many years earlier.

"I will only venture to say that I have never knowingly uttered a harsh or unkind word during any public controversy in which I have felt compelled to take a small part, and I certainly think it desirable that those who confess and call themselves Christians should not fall below that standard of courtesy which usually prevails among civilised human beings. As a matter of principle, however, I must assert my full right, if I see fit, to be a Radical, a Socialist (awful word!), a Disestablisher, and still claim my place as a clergyman and a Churchman, no fair-minded person who knows anything about the obligations of Churchmanship and the clerical office daring to say me nay.

Is it really possible in this twentieth century there are still to be found controversialists who will plainly declare that there is no room in one church for a clergyman unless he is a Conservative in politics and an upholder of an

Establishment which is outworn and visibly srangling some of the best possibilities of our religious life? I can only say that if such people exist, I, for my small part, will not give place to them-no, not for one hour".

He married Edith Lilian Prichard who had been born at Pwllywrach in 1864. Two more of our rivers had come together. Perhaps it was a surprising match for a left wing social reformer. As noted in an earlier chapter some member of the family had thought it worth playing "the John of Gaunt Game", preparing numerous sheets that set out to establish Mrs W.A. Edwards' royal and aristocratic ancestry. I cannot believe that her husband was much interested. My father was born at Pwllywrach in 1894 and my Aunt Averyl five years later in 1899. In 1908 my grandfather (referred to as Willie in my grandmother's scrapbook) became Rector of Abberffraw on the island of Anglesey, the small church among the sand dunes in the place that had been the seat of the Princes of Wales in medieval times. The parish was small with a population of only about 900. Two years later he suffered a breakdown in health and left Wales for Tredington, near Shipston-on-Stour in Warwickshire. I think that he must have had a nervous breakdown, perhaps partly as a result of the arguments about Disestablishment then approaching their climax. I also wonder whether my grandmother, coming from her county background in Glamorgan, may not have found the move to Anglesey uncongenial and increased the pressures on this sensitive man. After he moved to England, he did not lose his interest in public affairs, and he served on the Worcestershire County Council, having previously been a member of the Anglesey County Council. He was Rural-Dean of Shipston-on-Stour from 1921-1924. He retired from Tredington in 1926 and died in 1941.

The tributaries that lead down to my mother are very different. Francis Barbara van Rhenen from The Cape had married Lt. General Christopher Godby. Two of his daughters were to have marriages that would link the Godby tributary with the Brookes. First, Eliza Louisa married Major Charles Samuel Weston of the Bengal Army. Their daughter, Blanche, who was born in India, married Sir John Arthur Brooke Bt. from which union flow the Weston Brookes, some of whom still live at Midfearn Cottage at Bonnar Bridge in Scotland, although the present Baronet, Alistair, now lives in Wales. Eliza Louisa's youngest sister, Grace Charlotte, in 1859 married my great-grandfather, the Venerable Joshua Ingham Brooke, Archdeacon of Halifax, and Canon of Wakefield. There is also a third van Rhenen connection with the Brooke family, because an Aida Maria van Rhenen (1851-1937) married General Sir Thomas Hungerford Holditch, whose son, Brigadier General Harold Adrian Holditch (1874-1967) married Gertrude Elizabeth Brooke (1879-1967), the youngest sister of Thomas Brooke of Grimstone Manor, who was the father of Edward Brooke who ran the family business until the moment when it ceased the manufacture of cloth after the war and of Humphrey Brooke who was Secretary of the Royal Academy.

When, in the last chapter we were following the fortunes of the Brooke family in the 18th century, William, representing the tenth generation in the family business, was at Northgate House, Honley. His sons, John and Thomas, carried on the business and built Armitage Bridge Church. The family also paid a large part of the cost of reconstruction and refurbishment of the church of Saint Mary the Virgin at Honley, just down the road from Exchange House. Edward, the youngest son, was in his youth addicted to coursing and cock fighting, but went through a conversion so remarkable that he "could have got through the eye of the proverbial needle". He became a Methodist preacher, which may not have been entirely welcome to his high Anglican family. Thomas, also of Honley House, was born in 1798 and died in 1859. He married Ann, the daughter of Joseph Ingham. This was an alliance of prosperous Yorkshire families and introduced the name Ingham (about which we first heard in an earlier chapter) which was to become the name that identified another branch of the now large Brooke tribe.

A William Ingham had settled in Ossett, Yorkshire in the early part of the reign of Charles I and had died in 1670. Three further Williams, each the eldest son, followed in Ossett. The third of these five William Inghams of Osset had reached such a degree of prosperity that a younger son went to Oxford, but the father was still described as "plebeian" which was the 18th century way of saying that he was not of the gentry. Three quarters of a century later the descendants of the plebeian William are found established as woollen merchants and manufacturers in Leeds under the title of Ingham Bros & Co. The Oxford educated Benjamin, while still at the University, became associated with John Wesley and later in life was the founder of a religious sect known as the Inghamites. In 1741 he enhanced both his fortune and his social position by marrying the Lady Margaret Hastings, sister of the Earl of Huntingdon. The fifth William (who is said to have been a maltster) married a lady called Betty Fearnley, and their eldest son, Joseph, (1769-1846) was the senior partner of Ingham Bros & Co. He lived in Leeds and married Ann Hall. They had nine children, the last dying in 1798 at the age of one hundred. Their daughter, Ann, married Thomas Brooke, my great-grand-father.

The fourth son, William Bairstow Ingham, born in 1849, went out to Queensland in1872 with a reputed fortune of £60,000. He started a sugar plantation on the Herbert River, owned a paddle wheeled steamer and ran the first sawmill on the river. Later he was appointed a government resident in New Guinea. In 1878 he went to the Brooker Islands to make an inquiry about a murder. According to Raleigh Trevelyan in his book **Princes Under**

the Volcano, '*Some say that he was hustled overboard by natives and swam back laughing to his boat, others that he was wounded by a blow from a tomahawk and was thrown out to sea. At any rate when he grasped the gunwale, all his fingers were chopped off, and he was finished off with a spear as he struggled in the water. The rest of his crew were also massacred. Since the natives were cannibals, one can but draw conclusions about the fate of the corpses. The affair caused a great commotion in Queensland, where Ingham had been well esteemed. As a result a newly gazetted township on the Herbert River was named after him, a town which flourishes to this day.*

There is also a theory that he went to the islands to sell iron tanks, and that when he had his back turned the cannibals hit him on the head. 'They soon had him roasting on the fire' (letter to The Times 4 September 1929). A search party was sent to find him, but only the indigestible soles of his feet were left'.

At this point, having diverted to tell this sad tale, I cannot resist the temptation to follow another tributary stream in order to recount the remarkable story of the Ingham family's involvement with the Marsala wine trade and Sicily. Joseph Ingham, my great-great-great-grandfather, had by the first years of the eighteenth century, been joined in the business by his younger brother, Joshua. In the year 1806, Benjamin, a younger brother of Joseph and Joshua, was sent out to Sicily as a representative of Ingham Bros and Co. He was only 22 when he arrived in Sicily, but he was already a veteran of commercial ventures on his own account. He had been in Paris as early as 1802 after the Peace of Amiens, and before his arrival in Sicily had been involved in a venture that apparently had terminated with the loss of a ship in which most of his capital had been invested. There is a story told in the family that either Anne Brooke, the elder sister of my great-great grandfather, Thomas, had turned down Benjamin's proposal of marriage, or that her father had rejected his request that he should be allowed to marry his daughter on the grounds that his prospects were inadequate. It may have been that at 16 she was simply too young; but Massimo Brooke believed that the rejection may have represented a social and commercial change taking place at the turn of the 19th century. Textile merchants were at this time beginning to be overtaken by textile manufactures, in terms of wealth and status. Perhaps Ann's father already had his eye on Charles Brook who she eventually married in 1821. He was a representative of a family in control of more than one increasingly prosperous firm manufacturing cotton and silk sowing thread. Whatever the truth, the coincidence of a blighted romance and a business failure must have seemed a good enough reason for Benjamin to accept his brothers' proposal that he should represent them abroad.

It was a time when there was an urgent need for Yorkshire cloth merchants to find new markets. The war with Napoleon had closed most of the ports of Europe to trade with England, and there was increasing tension in the relations between Britain and the United States, a tension that was to lead to war in 1812. Sicily, under the friendly but forced occupation by British forces and defended by Nelson and the British fleet, represented a backdoor gateway to Europe for British trade. From Sicily the products of British industry and the British colonies were smuggled into the blockaded ports and along the coasts of the Mediterranean.

Benjamin quickly saw that there was more money to be made out of other things than cloth. In 1809 he was still acting as agent for his family's business, but he was also dealing on his own account, not only in cloth but in other English and colonial goods as well, and was exporting the produce of the island. In 1811 B. Ingham & Co appeared as one of thirteen British firms in Palermo petitioning the British consul to protest at a recently imposed Sicilian tax, and it would seem that by this time Ingham had a partner. This was probably the eccentric and difficult John Lee-Brown with whom there developed a most unhappy relationship. By 1817 Lee-Brown's conduct became wildly peculiar. One day he happened to meet Ingham in the Maqueda and started braying like a donkey. On another occasion he danced a Highland fling in Via Bara outside Ingham's counting house; and 'he adorned his hat with peacocks' feathers, torn from the tails of the unfortunate birds owned by the Princess of Palagonia'. It is not surprising that he would be replaced by a string of nephews who could be harried and directed by an uncle who kept tight control over every aspect of the business.

Benjamin Ingham had very quickly recognised the potential of the new trade in marsala wine. Marsala, as a fortified wine, had been developed by a John Woodhouse who added grape spirit to the wine and after an initial trial shipped the first large batch to England in 1773. Its initial popularity was reinforced when Nelson ordered a large quantity for the British fleet. Woodhouse opened his first warehouse (*baglio*) and cellars in 1796. Benjamin was not the first to attempt to follow Woodhouse's example, but he prepared the ground more carefully and before committing himself to the Marsala venture he arranged for his brother, Joshua, to visit Spain and Portugal, to discover the methods employed there in fortifying wines, and to study the marketing methods of the most successful producers. With his preparations complete, in 1812 Benjamin opened a *baglio* almost next to Woodhouse's and entered into competition with him. In 1833 Vicenzo Florio was to open a third *baglio*. For the next one hundred years the three firms ruled the industry until, in 1929, Cinzano bought them.

According to a contemporary observer, '*the.... enclosures of the [Ingham] Baglio, with its high blank windowless wall, and its loopholed towers...gave more the impression of a fortified post, than a wine establishment*'. The walls of the two *baglii* enclosed a very large area, and the premises contained not only the buildings in which the wine was processed and the vaults where it was stored, but also flower and vegetable gardens, poultry yards, and even fields of wheat and small vineyards. The Ingham *baglio* also contained a house where Benjamin lived for a number of years. The wife of a later occupant remembered it as a rather uncomfortable place *'with the trying fumes of the fermented grapes and the noise of the workers, hammering at the cooperage, and rolling out the heavy barrels of wine...'*; but others recalled many delightful evenings when the Englishmen of the *baglio* and their ladies sat on the wide wall above the gate enjoying the cool breeze that blew in from the sea. On a visit to Sicily Ann and I found it still standing, though sadly in a semi-ruinous state. Raleigh Trevelyan describes it as *'a handsome place. Almost the scale of a colonial mansion in Virginia, it is flat-roofed with two stories. A portico runs the length of the building down-stairs, to provide shade, while the first floor has seven French windows leading on to a balustraded balcony with eight pairs of columns. In front is a large courtyard , which used to have arcades along each side'*.

The business grew rapidly and Benjamin began to trade with America. He visited Boston in 1809 to appoint suitable agents. America may have been chosen partly to avoid direct competition with Woodhouse during the early years of the marsala venture. Although wine was initially the principal product, sulphur was also shipped in ballast, and the firm also sent rags, sumac, and olive oil to England to make up cargo and fill the ships. Benjamin quickly branched into diversified activities as a ship owner, trader, and banker. Although many of the records of the business were destroyed during the Allied bombing of Palermo in 1943, fortunately 'a vast pile' of Benjamin Ingham's business letter-books from 1816 to 1860 were placed in safety at the beginning of the war. From them, Raleigh Trevelyan extracted a great deal of information about the business.

To assist him, in 1816 Benjamin first brought out from Yorkshire his nephew, William Whitaker (aged 20), one of the sons of his sister Mary. In the same year Lee-Brown had recruited an earnest young man called Richard Stephens, who a year later was to replace him and in 1826 become a partner of the Marsala business. Sadly in 1819 William Whitaker died of a fever. There is a story that soon after William's death Benjamin Ingham wrote to the young man's mother, his sister: 'Your son is dead. Send me another'. The story is probably untrue. These were troubled times in Sicily and Mary cannot have been entirely happy about sending her eighteen year old son, Joseph, to take the place of his elder brother. None-the-less she agreed, and Joseph reached Palermo around 1820. Though dour, he was a perfect desk man and ran the 'Concern' so well that in due course he would take over from his uncle its management and become a partner in the business. He started a line of Anglo

Sicilian grandees about whom we shall hear more. Later in the century and after Benjamin's death the Whitakers were to take over the business from their Ingham cousins; but that event was still some time off.

In 1823 Benjamin Ingham paid a visit to England, and while in Leeds recruited yet another nephew to work in Sicily. He chose another Joseph, an Ingham this time, a rather lugubrious individual, born in 1811. He was to be followed a year or two later by Benjamin, born in 1810 and Joshua, born in 1811. These Inghams were the brothers of my great-great grandmother, Ann, born in 1809. Benjamin also discussed the possibility of persuading another young Joshua Ingham to join his cousins in the 'Concern'. This was the Joshua Ingham of Blake Hall who employed Anne Bronte. Probably because he was well enough off on his own account, with the prospect of estates to manage in Yorkshire, he was not tempted by the offer of a job in Sicily.

With the arrival of the Joshua that had chosen to come, Joseph was sent off to Boston to take charge of the rapidly expanding American business, although the words 'take charge', hardly represents the true situation because he was deluged with letters and instructions from his uncle. After Joseph's departure, Joshua (1811-1846) lived at the *baglio*, managing the concern in his uncle's absence. Benjamin Ingham, (who, at least until the time of the elder Ingham's death, always referred to himself as "Benjamin Ingham, Jr." and was known in the family as Ben) married Emily Hinton, and died without children in 1872. His widow was afterwards to marry a General Giacoma Medici, and there are stories told about attempts by members of the Medici family to recover jewellery that had got into the hands of the Inghams. However, those goings on, if they happened at all, were far into the future. Beginning in the 1830's and continuing into the 1860's, Benjamin Jr. made frequent trips to England and America, and after his brother Joshua's death in 1846 seems to have managed the Marsala business during those periods when he was in Sicily.

By the 1830's, then, the elder Benjamin had so arranged things that he had one nephew looking after his interests in Marsala, another to serve as second in command in Palermo, a third to send on roving commissions, and Joseph in the port of Boston in the United States. Joseph arrived in Boston at least as early as 1828. Although Joseph was a merchant on his own account, a great part of his time was devoted to looking after his uncle's affairs. Benjamin kept his nephew to the grindstone. With the market growing so rapidly he could not let him relax; but on the 8 October 1833 Joseph committed suicide at the City Hotel, New York. The Coroner's verdict was that the suicide was due to melancholy. We know that in August he had suffered a 'deplorable accident' in Boston, but what it was we do not know. There was some dispute about the will, and Ben (Benjamin Jr) was sent to investigate these sad events. He remained in America for the next two years.

Ben was largely responsible for adding a substantial trade in citrus fruits to the activities of the firm. From as early as 1807 small quantities of lemons and oranges had been shipped from Sicily to the United States, and by 1834 Ingham and Co. had become involved in a modest way. In 1835, while in America, Ben took it upon himself to commit the firm to a quite large speculative venture in fruit, and from that time on the firm remained deeply involved in the fruit trade with the United States.

By the 1830's The elder Benjamin, who was later to be described as the 'English Croesus'. was easily the richest man in Sicily. According to his biographer, Tina Whitaker, writing ninety-nine years later, in 1837 he married Alessandra Spadofara, Duchess of Santa Rosalia. He was already in his 53rd year and she was a widow with four sons. It seems likely that they had been on intimate terms for some years and Tina refers to Benjamin choosing the occasion of his marriage to "regularise his position" with "his friend" the Duchess. Raleigh Trevelyan asserts that *'Whatever form the ceremony took, there are plenty of reasons for supposing that the marriage between the Duchess and her 'cicisbeo' was never made legal'.* Benjamin, however, refers to the Duchess as his beloved wife and he probably went through some form of civil formula.

Benjamin's wealth did not simply arise from his business in Sicily. As we have seen he traded extensively with the United States, and there he invested his profits in coal, railways, and real estate. In 1853 the nine short railways that crossed New York state were consolidated into one system, the New York Central Railroad. Benjamin already had large holdings in the smaller lines and these were exchanged for stock in the new corporation. In the 1850's his agent continued to purchase New York Central stocks and bonds and by 1860 his investment in the Central amounted to $640,000 or about 3% of the total stock. He invested in other railroads, in a ship canal company, and land in the vicinity of New York City, purchasing it at "agricultural prices" and selling it at "building value". It is said that he owned part of what is now Fifth Avenue. It was not just the profits from the trade with America that was invested there but also the profits from the very much larger trade with Britain and Europe.

After those early years in the *baglio* in Marsala he lived in Palermo, first in the Piano di Sant' Oliva and then at the Palazzo Ingham, which later, in an enlarged form, was to become the Grand Hotel des Palmes where Wagner completed *Parsifal* on June 14th 1882. Tina Whitaker, about whom we will soon learn more, used to sing for Wagner, but was irritated by the way Cosima would throw different coloured veils over the Master according to his supposed moods. When Garibaldi was advancing on Palermo, Benjamin and his wife refused to be evacuated for safety to one of the British warships outside the harbour. It is said that after the fighting had begun, the aged Duchess, on spotting a Bourbon soldier cutting down one of her precious new palm trees for a barricade, ran out and banged him on the head with a bottle of Marsala. Benjamin had announced his retirement in 1851, ten years before his death. He issued a statement that the business which had been carried on in Palermo *under the Firm of B. Ingham and Co. will be continued by Joseph Whitaker under the firm of Ingham and Whitaker'.* Joshua had died in 1846. Benjamin's "retirement" was in name rather than in fact, and he continued active in the business until his death in 1861. In those years he evidently found time to cast his mind back to the circumstances of his blighted romance before his arrival in Sicily in 1806. In a letter to his sister Ann, dated 19th and 27th January, 1853, Benjamin Jun. refers to the old man and states that "he asked many questions about you and your family. He enquired about his old sweetheart (as he calls Mrs Charles...)." Benjamin may have reflected that if he had been turned down because his prospects were poor, he had not done too badly!

Joseph Whitaker's son, Will, was the eventual heir of the bulk of Benjamin Ingham Senior's fortune; but Benjamin left £4000 to his niece Ann, my great-great grandmother, and a life interest in his Estate to her brother Benjamin Jr. (Ben) who died in 1872 in Paris. Raleigh Trevelyan wrongly states that Ben's English estate was less than £40,000. It was, in fact, a little under £400,000. (I have a copy of the will) The Palermo House and its contents went to his widow, Emily, and there were various other bequests. Of the remainder, £30,000 went to each of Ann's five sons (one of them was my great-grandfather, Joshua Ingham Brooke), and £10,000 each to her six surviving daughters; and a half interest in the Ossett estate to her elder son, Thomas. That, on the basis of its Rent Roll in 1858-59, would have been worth at least £10,000.

The story of the business in Sicily now becomes the story of the Whitakers, and in particular the descendants of Joseph. Just as more than one generation of Brookes married Inghams, so did Inghams marry Whitakers. Isaac Whitaker of Baghill (1684-1750) married Susannah Ingham and his grandson Joseph (1770-1820) married Mary, the daughter of William Ingham of Ossett. It was their sons, William and Joseph, who arrived in Sicily to work for Mary's brother Benjamin. Joseph (1802-1804) married Sophia Sanderson, the daughter of the British Consul in Messina, and built Villa Sophia in her honour on a hill just outside Palermo. Of Joseph and Sophia Whitaker's twelve children, only three remained in Sicily for long: Joshua, known as Joss; Robert, known as Bob; and Joseph Isaac, known as Pip, although Will, Benjamin's main heir, was still living in a villa in Palermo by the Piazza Castelnuovo in the late 1860s. He had the pretty little bandstand in the square built to protect his view. Bob and his wife Euphrosyne Manuel, the owner of a famous collection of corals from Trampani, built the Villa Whitaker, a Gothic Venetian style palace, which later became the Prefettura or police headquarters. The exotic-looking Effie was half Maltese and known in Palermo as Signora Whitaker Papagallo, because she went about with a parrot on her shoulder.

In 1883 Pip married Tina (Caterina) Scalia (the lady who was to sing for Wagner). She was half Sicilian, half Tuscan, but born as she used to say 'in exile' in London, being the daughter of Risorgimento patriot refugees. Her father had distinguished himself as a General in Garibaldi's campaigns. She was a diarist and writer, very socially ambitious and trained as an opera singer. Her great moment came when she sang with the tenor Tamagno at the Politeama in Palermo. Pip was an amateur archaeologist, ornithologist and botanist. Between 1885 and 1886 Pip and Tina bought almost ten hectares of land at Malfitano and commissioned the architect Ignazio Greco to build an immensely splendid villa. It was lavishly furnished and decorated, and despite a bad fire in 1994, stands to-day in splendour in a garden of exceptional richness and interest. The garden contains a large variety of trees and palms, including a huge *Ficus Magnoloides,* and plants from Tunisia, Sumatra, Chile, Australia and Mexico. An enormous wisteria and climbing roses cover one side of the house. Tina Whitaker gave a ball at Malfitano for The German Kaiser and her sons; entertained Edward VII and Queen Alexandra in 1907; and, in 1925, welcomed George V and Queen Mary.

Pip acquired the island of Motya in order to carry out archaeological work on the important Phoenician site that had been discovered there. He published a book about it in 1921 and built the museum which has since been enlarged and modernised and contains a particularly fine Phoenician sculpture recovered from the sea. Pip died in 1936 but Tina lived on to 1957 when she died aged nearly 99. There were two daughters; Norina who, after being courted by practically every eligible bachelor in Sicily, in middle age married General Sir Antonio di Giogio, GCVO, KCMG, who despite his English honours was for a short time Mussolini's war minister. He died in 1932. Delia (the last of the Whitakers in Sicily) never married. Tina, Norina and Delia were in Rome throughout the war, until on 4 June 1944 Rome was liberated and a visitor was announced, as Delia's diary records: '*It was Captain Brooke, a distant cousin. He had just come from Cassino and two months ago had landed in Sicily on a special Allied commission for the protection of Italian art treasures. He gave us the first news of Malfitano that we had had for so long'.* This was Humphrey Brooke, who later became Secretary of the Royal Academy. Before Delia died in 1977, aged 86, she offered Malfitano to the

British government; but the offer was turned down. Instead, she created the *Fondazione Guiseppe Whitaker* in memory of her father, 'to promote the study of Punic-Phoenician culture in the Mediterranean'. The house and island of Motya are now the property of the Foundation. Raleigh Trevelyan (in the *Companion Guide to Sicily)* describes Delia as 'a sweet-natured woman'. 'Her presence is strongly felt at Malfitano by those who knew her, especially in the garden room where she loved to sit, stroking her ancient cat Pellegrina'. Her gift and creation of the Foundation was a happy conclusion to an extraordinary story.

While I was researching this part of the family history, I suddenly realised that The Baroness Whitaker, sitting on the Labour benches opposite me also had a link to this tale. Her husband, the former Labour MP, Ben Whitaker, is a grandson of Pip's youngest brother Albert and great-grandson of the Joseph Whitaker who took over the management of the business with such efficiency from his uncle Benjamin. He is also my fourth cousin (once removed). As I reminded him, the Whitakers had inherited a great deal more than the Brookes from Uncle Benjamin. "Whitaker wealth is not a subject that I like to talk to my Labour friends about", he remarked; "but what a pity we don't still own part of Fifth Avenue"!

We now return to the Brookes and the descendants of Thomas Brooke and Ann Ingham. The eldest brother of William and the Archdeacon was Sir Thomas Brooke, the first and last Baronet of Armitage Bridge, who collected a library that contained many famous books. The youngest brother was Charles Edward Brooke, the Vicar of St. John the Divine, Kennington, a magnificent Victorian church which he had built and largely financed. *Charles Edward Brooke--A Memoir* by Arthur Gordon Deedes, first published in 1912 gives us a picture of the Brookes as they were in the mid 19th century.

"Charles Edward Brooke ....was born at Northgate House, Honley, in the neighbourhood of Huddersfield, on July 9, 1847. He was the youngest of thirteen, five sons and eight daughters, all of whom were living at the time of his birth. His father was Thomas Brooke, head of the firm of John Brooke and Sons, who were well-known cloth manufacturers in that part of Yorkshire. His mother, Ann, belonged to the family of Ingham, and was born at Hunslet near Leeds--thus from both parents Yorkshire blood was flowing through his veins. To this fact we may trace some of those characteristic features in the shape of strength, sturdiness and hospitality which were stamped upon his after-years.

All four of his brothers made their mark in life, and their names have become almost household names in the North, not only for their boundless generosity, their devotion to the cause of Christ's Church, and their interest in all good works. The eldest, Sir Thomas Brooke, was for many years a director of the London and North-Western Railway. Mr William and Mr John Arthur Brooke are certainly to

be ranked among the most influential and widely respected laymen in their county;
while the remaining brother, Ingham, became Vicar and Archdeacon of Halifax,
in which capacity he served his parish and diocese in such a way as to earn the
affection and confidence of all with whom he was brought into contact..........
Both parents were undoubtedly devout people, evangelical in their views, who
nowadays would be described as puritanical. All such pastimes as cards, dances,
and theatres, would be rigidly eschewed, while Sunday would be spent with an
almost Sabbatical severity. The Bible and the Church Catechism were diligently
taught, to the total exclusion of all books except such as were of a distinctly narrow
religious type. It would never have entered the head of any member of the family
to absent himself from the public worship of the Church, or to indulge in any of
those Sunday employments which would in these days be regarded as perfectly
pardonable".

It is perhaps not surprising that Charles Edward, although deeply devout, became a high churchman rather than an evangelical puritan; and Ingham, too, was, I believe, much less austere in his approach. A son of Ingham, the Archdeacon, was to marry a Wallich and we now, therefore have to return to the start of the century and the young Danish surgeon at Serampore, a Dutch settlement in India. In 1808 Serampore fell into the hands of the East India Company; and in 1809, after a brief spell as a prisoner of war, Nathaniel Wallich with other officers, were allowed to enter the English service. On 30 May 1812 Nathaniel married Julane Marie Hals who was subsequently known to the English as Mary Ann. She was only 14. And she died only two months later. Her memorial was placed in the Danish church in Serampore:

"Sacred to the Memory of Mary Ann Wallich, she was born September 19th, 1797, and married May 30th, 1812, to N. Wallich. She died August 1st, 1812. Farewell, but not for ever, How unavailing her blooming youth, the spotless innocence of her character, the universal esteem she enjoyed, the fondness of her affectionate husband, to arrest the arm of death".

My cousin David Brooke who obtained this information during his researches into the Wallichs, speculated in rather dramatic terms about these events; but the wording suggests tragedy and not scandal. I told him that I was not as surprised as he was that Nathaniel's bride should have been so young. At a time when the number of European women in India was very small and many European men had Indian wives or partners, it was probably not unusual for women to marry very young. Women tend to mature early in the tropics, or so my mother-in-law used to tell Ann (and her family had been Far East Indian traders for over 100 years). In William Dalrymple's book White Mughals there are references to Indian brides of 15. For a time

Nathaniel left India and went to Mauritius. Perhaps this was because of shock and grief, but his health was never strong, and his need for a period in which to recover his strength does not seem surprising. He was not away for long, and in 1813 he married Sophia (Sophie) Collings, the second daughter of Leonard Collings. They had seven children, two of whom died in infancy

Nathaniel Wallich had been a pupil of Professor Martin Vahl, the author of *Symbolae botanicae* (1790-04), at the University of Copenhagen and, although first attached to the medical staff, in 1815 he was made superintendent of the Calcutta botanical garden. He was to become one of the greatest botanists of the 19th century. He quickly became an avid collector of new plants, distributing specimens to the chief English gardens and herbaria. Other parts of the world, too, were indebted to his generosity and skill, and to the network of official and unofficial collectors that he employed and fostered.

His own collection is now in the herbarium at Kew, where during a visit in 2003 I inspected some of the specimens in it from the year 1828, clearly labelled in Nathaniel's own hand. Other botanists shared in the labour and rewards of distribution. One of them, George Bentham, rejoiced in the company "of Joyous Wallich" and his oyster lunches. "Generous, liberal and expansive", he relished every moment of his philanthropic mission. One of his obituaries acknowledged that "there was scarcely an English garden of magnitude, which was not indebted to his liberality". He suffered a good deal from ill-health and he could be volatile, impetuous, difficult and even vindictive; but his botanic competence was widely recognised and he earned the support of, among others, Sir Joseph Banks (who Nathaniel subsequently showered with gifts of plants in gratitude); the Governor General, The Marquis of Hastings; and Field Marshall, Sir George Nugent, Bt whose remarkable career will shortly earn him a note of his own.

In 1820 Nathaniel was officially directed to explore Nepal; and in 1825 he inspected the forests of Western Hindustan, and in 1826 and 1827 those of Ava and Lower Burmah. A passenger on the first steamboat to navigate the Irrawaddy, he botanised with satisfactory results whenever the ship moored. Invalided home in 1828, he brought with him some eight thousand specimens of plants. I n 1830, 1831, and 1832 he produced the most important of a considerable number of publications, *Plantae Asiaticae Rariores; or Descriptions and Figures of a Select Number of unpublished East Indian Plants. (London, 3 vols,folio)*. In the Royal Society's Catalogue, he is credited with twenty-one papers, mostly botanical between 1816 and 1854.

Nathaniel Wallich returned to India, where, among other official duties, he made an extensive journey in Assam to find out more about the wild tea shrub. The discovery that the tea plant grows wild in Assam had been reported as early as 1815; and in 1823 Robert Bruce observed tea plants growing in the hills. In about 1826 some leaves of these plants reached Wallich in Calcutta, but with leaves only as evidence he was cautious and provisionally identified them as a species of Camellia. In 1832 a Tea Committee was set up, and in 1835 it arranged for Wallich to lead an expedition to Assam to investigate the possibility of tea cultivation. As a result of the report that he produced tea was in the course of time to become the major income producing crop of Assam. Among other journeys were those to the East Indies and Singapore, where he advised Sir Stamford Raffles, with whom he later corresponded, and to the Cape, where he spent two years between 1842 and 1844. He finally returned to England in 1847, ill and worn out after 40 arduous years' employment in India.

The fullest account of Nathaniel Wallich's life and work is to be found in *The European Discovery of the Indian Flora* by Ray Desmond. Among his numerous contributions to English gardens are cotoneasters-*frigidus, microphyllus* and *rotundifolius;* several species of geranium--*lambertii, nepalense* and *wallichianum; bergenia ligulata,* and *pinus wallichiana.* He discovered the giant lily, *cardiocrinum giganteum,* introduced into England by Edward Madden in 1848. He was confident that most rhododendrons would adapt to the British climate*: Rhododendron formosum* was one of his early discoveries.

William Carey, the missionary, saw him as 'a man of great warmth [but] perhaps too lively in his resentment'. Thomas Hardwick cautioned him not to allow 'the irritability of his temper to outreach his reason'. He had many admirers, but he made enemies and had numerous clashes with those with whom he worked and employed. He finally returned to England in In 1847; and on his resignation of his post at the botanic garden in 1850, he was succeeded by John Scott, gardener to the Duke of Devonshire at Chatsworth. As vice-president of the Linnean Society, where his portrait by Lucas hangs to-day in its premises in Burligton House, he frequently presided over its meetings in his later years. He was elected a fellow of the Royal Society in 1829, and was also a fellow of the Royal Asiatic Society. He died in London in 1854. An obelisk was erected to his memory by the East India Company in the botanical garden in Calcutta. His name was applied by several botanists to various genera of plants; but the admitted genus *Wallichia* is a group of palms named by William Roxburgh. As a child I used to enjoy hunting for plants labelled *Wallichia* in Kew Gardens.

Once again I cannot resist a diversion, this time to record the extraordinary career of Sir George Nugent, Bt. who had so warmly supported Nathaniel Wallich. Born in 1757, he served in eight different regiments, one of which he raised himself. He saw action in America between 1777 and 1783, and in the Netherlands in 1793. Despite being appointed to the Irish Staff and holding commands in various parts of Ireland between 1794 and 1801, a period that covered the Irish Rebellion, he sat in the House of Commons from 1790 to 1800, and between 1799 and 1801 represented Charleville, County Cork, in the last Irish Parliament. From 1801 to 1806 he was Commander-in-Chief in Jamaica. He was back in the English House of Commons again in the 1806-1807 Parliament. He was Commander-in-Chief in India in 1811-1813, becoming a full General in 1813. Back in England, he was again an MP from 1812 until the passing of the Reform Bill in 1830. He was made a Field-Marshal in 1846, and died in 1849, aged 92. It seems surprising that against a background of such a remarkable career he should have remembered the young Nathaniel Wallich and referred to him in his reminiscences. No doubt he met him during his time as Commander-in-Chief of The East India Company forces in India, when the Danish settlement at Serampore fell into the hands of the Company and the young surgeon, with other officers, was allowed to enter the English service.

As we discovered, earlier, Nathaniel married Sophie Collings (his second wife) and they had seven children. Their son, George Charles Wallich was born in Calcutta, educated at King's College, Aberdeen and the University of Edinburgh where he graduated as a doctor in 1836, became a surgeon in 1837, and entered the Indian Medical Service in 1838. He received medals for his services in the Sutlej and Punjab campaigns of 1842 and 1847, and was field-surgeon during the Sonthal rebellion in 1855-6. During his 19 years of military service in India he only returned to England once, in 1850. It was while he was there in 1851 that he married, and it was on the voyages to and from India that he first showed an interest in the science of oceanography to which he was to make a distinguished contribution. In 1860 he was attached to *HMS Bulldog* on her historic survey of the Atlantic bottom with the object of finding a more suitable route for the Atlantic cable than that of the first cable which had been laid in 1858. For more than twenty years he continued to study marine biology. In 1860, after the Bulldog voyage, he published *Notes on the Presence of Animal Life at Great Depths in the Ocean* and in 1862 *The North Atlantic Sea-bed.*. He received the gold medal of the Linnean Society for his researches. He died in 1899.

A large batch of his papers in the Wellcome Library and an article in The Journal of the Society for the History of Natural History Entitled G.C. Wallich *M.D- megalomaniac or misused oceanographic genius?* provide the sources for a portrait of this unusual man. The collection in the Wellcome Library centres on his work on marine biology, and his belief that the other figures in the field at the time were ignoring or plagiarising his discoveries. S. A. J. Moorat, who compiled the catalogue of manuscripts in the Wellcome Library, wrote "He undoubtedly laboured under a strong sense of grievance and injustice, which seems to have increased as he grew older: for he believed that his discoveries had from the first been deliberately ignored, and later stolen or plagiarised". At the time of the departure of the *Bulldog* it was widely accepted that life could not exist under the extraordinary conditions of pressure, light, and temperature prevailing in the great depths of the sea. The most famous version of this idea was known as the "azoic theory", developed by Edward Forbes during the 1830s and 1840s. George Wallich claimed that his own work on the *Bulldog* had proved this theory wrong and "that the presence of a living fauna in the deeper abysses of the ocean had been fully established". This judgement was not immediately accepted by the rest of the scientific community, and it was not until the cruises of the *Porcupine in 1869* that the adherents of the "azoic" theory abandoned the idea. The cruise of the *Bulldog* is now largely forgotten, and it was to be overtaken in importance by the voyage of *HMS Challenger* (1872-76). It was the fact that honours were showered on the main *Challenger* personalities while his own work was ignored that seems to have principally stimulated his frustration and fury. In George Wallich's view the chief offenders were Henry Clfton Sorby (1826-1908), geologist, Sir Charles Wyvill Thomson (1825-1850), naturalist, and William Benjamin Carpenter (1813-1885), physician and naturalist. He had a bitter dislike of Thomas Henry Huxley, whom he considered a plagiarist and charlatan; but his particular hatred was aimed at Carpenter whom he described as "Fur" (Thief).

The contrast between the language and tone of his numerous publications in learned journals and the later personal notes is striking. The arguments advanced in the publications, though verbose, are clearly presented and are supported by a wealth of material about the nature of the seabed and the living organisms that he found in the ocean. The notebooks and the hand written annotations on some of the printed material are very frequently hysterical in tone, and it is evident that during the later years of his life George Wallich was a bitter and very angry man. There are allegations of slander, libel and plagiarism and many references to "lies and gross lies". The detailed criticisms of the opinions of the other scientists are often supported by quotations from his own publications such as *North Atlantic Sea Bed, 1863*, a paper read to the Royal Geographical Society in 1863, and an article on the *North Atlantic Sea-bed* in the Quarterly Journal of Science for January 1864. When, in 1898, one of his sons received the Linnean Society's Gold Medal on his behalf "in recognition of his researches into the problems connected with bathybial and pelagial life", it was probably too little and too late to satisfy the old man. That November he wrote the pathetic observation "If any man ever was for forty years a victim of such a set of scoundrels, I am that man". Four months later "he died, bitter and frustrated to the end".

The three authors of the article that has been my other source, A. L. Rice, Harold. L. Burstyn and A. G. E. Jones conclude "It is difficult to say whether Wallich was justified in feeling so much resentment towards the scientific establishment of his day and towards Carpenter and Wyvile Thomson in particular. His early work, and especially that arising from the *Bulldog* cruise did not, perhaps, receive the recognition that it deserved, but on the other hand he seems to have lacked either the good fortune or the ability to carry any major task to a definite conclusion".

"*Finally, he would almost certainly have progressed further up the scientific ladder if he had been a less prickly character, and less ready to take offence, and also if his literary style had been somewhat less cumbersome. For the combination of his verbosity and his egotism is a formidable deterrent to a serious consideration of his work, and it was almost certainly easier to dismiss his later works as those of a crank, rather than be drawn into his detailed pedantic arguments.*

In all things Wallich seems to have made a great deal out of very little. His sensitivity made him over-react to the words of others so that he could see a well-aimed blow in a casual remark, and at the same time he often extrapolated from his own results to draw conclusions which were hardly justified. But these conclusions were more often right than wrong, and perhaps his most fitting epitaph was written by Murray, one of his arch enemies, in the Summary volume of the Challenger Reports-- 'many of Wallich's opinions have been confirmed by subsequent researches, and altogether he must be regarded as one of the most industrious pioneers in the investigation of the deep-sea'." That seems a fair judgement of my great-grandfather's contribution to science.

Surgeon Major George Charles Wallich married Caroline Elizabeth Norton in 1851 during that leave from military service in India. She was baptised in 1828 at Lowestoft in Suffolk. Her father, Edmund Norton, who appears to have been a solicitor, married Sophia Louisa Palmer. The baptismal and marriage records tell us that there was an Edmund Norton, born in 1741, who married Mary Randall at Castleton in Dorset, an Edmund Norton baptised in 1645 at Stamford in Lincolnshire, and before that a Thomas Norton who married a lady called Anne. However the links with those earlier Nortons are not clearly established and so we can only guess at the source of this particular stream. Caroline appears to have had two brothers, George William Norton and Edmund Palmer Norton, and an Edmund Scott Norton, baptised in 1864 may have been a nephew. The Wallichs had eight children: my grandmother, Beatrice Harriet was born in 1859, a year before the voyage of the Bulldog; there were three sisters; Alice who died in 1892; Edith who worked in the slums and lived in Rotherhithe; and Elinor, who I used to visit as a child in Oxford and who was very religious in the days when I knew her. There were four sons; Charly was a tea planter who was drowned at Hearne

Bay! Collings (I have letters from him to my grandmother about their father) who went to British Columbia and had a family, where many years later, he welcomed my first cousin, Anne Minard (neé Brooke), who was still in her early twenties and had made a remarkable journey across the continent at a time when journeys of that kind were more difficult and unusual than they are today. According to Anne, Collings' son became a Jehovah's Witness and his daughter, more English than the English, ran a gift shop. Marmaduke went to Australia; and Horace who was a not very good artist lived most of his life in Russia. I remember him as a cantankerous old man who we used to collect from his old peoples' home to spend Christmas day with us in Chiswick. My cousin, Vanora Bennett, in her book *The Taste of Dreams* (headline Book Publishing, 2003), devotes a chapter to the discoveries that she made about Horace's life while he was in Russia. She found a reference to him in a book about Fabergé for whom he seems to have worked as a miniaturist. For a time he lived in St Petersburg in a flat on Bolshaya Konyushennaya Street, which ran from the Winter Palace's enormous stable block to Nevsky Prospekt; and in the book he is listed as one of ten miniature painters employed by the St Petersburg branch of Fabergé. There are other references in official records to Goras Volik, painter, and to Goratsy Vallikh, a miniaturist. Vanora suggests that information obtained from the UK census of 1881 provides a clue as to why he had gone to Russia. Apparently, the Wallich males in their south London home had with them a Bengali law student, an elderly lunatic lady in the attic who was Surgeon Major George Charles Wallich's patient, and "a clutch of stolid-sounding servants from Kent". A Russian family lived next door with a governess, cook and nurse. There was a ten-year-old daughter, Wera, born in St Petersburg. Vanora writes: "I began to imagine the two children playing in each other's suburban gardens, and a small Horace spellbound by Wera's and her mother's soulful voices, their icons, their glittering trinkets and nostalgia for palaces and snow. I have no way of knowing what had happened between then and the moment, twenty nine years later, when forty-year-old Horace reached St Petersburg (though I liked to think that he might have married Wera)". It is, of course, all speculation, as is her conclusion, reached on the grounds that the neighbours listed on the same page sounded poorer and less educated, that the Wallich family had fallen on hard times. I will return to that subject when I have finished the story of great-uncle Horace. I will only observe at this point that I wish I had asked more questions when Horace came to those Christmas lunches and when my mother would have known the answers.

The Fabergé business was destroyed by the Russian revolution, and a hand written note in the book that stimulated Vanora's researches, probably written by my Aunt Faith, recorded that Wallich and his wife "got off from Yalta in a British vessel, *Princess Ina* or *Ena* to Malta and thus to 'peace and plenty'. Then after some weeks they were brought by 13,000 tonner to Southampton and London". Among others who took the same route were the Tsar's mother, the Dowager Empress, and Prince Dmitry Obolensky, whose son, Dmitry Obolensky, a distinguished British academic who was only one at the time, described their adventures in his memoirs. The Obolenskys waited in Yalta for six months and watched the war between the Red and White Russians; but when the Bolsheviks broke through, capturing Kiev and Odessa in October 1919, they and other aristocratic refugees in Yalta were hastily evacuated by British and French ships. The grandest nobility, led by the Dowager Empress (sister of the Queen of England), set sail on *HMS Marlborough*. The infant Dmitri and his mother were given places on a British transport ship travelling with the *Marlborough*, the *Princess Ena*. They set off through heavy seas for Sevastapol, where Dmitri's father joined the family, and on the night of 10 April the ships left Russia for ever. Horace Wallich may have watched the departure of the Dowager Empress, and he certainly accompanied the Obolenskys for part of the journey that took them to England. Perhaps the sad and rather bitter old man that I knew years later felt, like his father before him, that life had not treated him well and that his talents had not been adequately recognised.

The 1881 census that stimulated Vanora's imaginative ideas about Horace also prompts a different question. It reveals that at that time Caroline (age 53) was living with three of her daughters, Alice (age 24), Edith (age 19), and Elinor (age 18), at 47 Norland Square. She is described as a lodging house keeper, but as two of the daughters, Edith and Elinor, are described as Kinder Garten teachers it seems likely that the house was part of the Norland Nursery business that had been started by Emily Ward, the Wardy or "Great Originator" of the caravan adventure which we will hear about shortly. The census describes her as Proprietress and Teacher of Kinder Garten and informs us that she was living round the corner at 9 and 10 Norland Place, as was Caroline's fourth daughter, my grandmother, Beatrice (age 21). However, Caroline's husband, George Charles Wallich, then aged 65, was at 3 and 4 Christchurch Road, Lambeth with three of their four sons, Collings (age 16), Marmaduke (age 13) and Horace (age 11). We do not know where Charly, the fourth son, was that night. We, therefore, have an unexplained mystery: why were the family not all living in the same house? It is, I suppose, possible that by 1881 the marriage had broken down and that my great-grandparents were living apart. The bitter and obsessed old man revealed by the Wellcome Library papers would not have been easy to live with. However, it is equally possible that there was a perfectly straightforward reason why on census night the male members of the family were all at a different address from the women, who may have all been busy with the Kinder Garten business. It would be nice to know, and once again I am left regretting that I did not start to ask questions such as these until after my mother's generation were no longer alive to provide the answers.

My grand-mother, Beatrice, must have been a spirited young woman at the time of her marriage. In her twenties she had led a life that in the 1880s would have been regarded as unconventional. To give one example, she and a number of other young men and women undertook a quite extensive tour of southern England in a gipsy caravan. Their adventures were recorded in a charming book entitled *How They Enjoyed Themselves* published in 1890 by The Women's Printing Society in Great College Street, Westminster. It identified the members of the party, several of whom contributed chapters, simply by their initials or by nicknames. (My grandmother was Polypa, "sometimes irreverently alluded to as 'Polly'"); and its dedication, in the form of a poem, contains a verse which confirms that they recognised their unconventional behaviour:

> *What of conventional customs and curious*
> *Kept by a narrow though well meaning clique?*
> *What of its judgements of "Frantic and furious",*
> *Those were the words. Are they wise? Are they weak?*

Among the party was the Rev. William Ingham Brooke, the second of the nine children of the Archdeacon of Halifax. I assume that he was of the party because three of the letters of congratulations retained by Granny, tucked within the covers of the book, refer to the perils of caravanning! I suspect that he was "the Cadger" who was "always cheery" and "enjoyed the friendship of every tramp from Cornwall to the Shetlands, and consequently was useful in keeping the peace with them *en route*". Despite the close proximity of companions, the journey evidently provided suitable opportunities for courting, and my grandparents became engaged in 1890 not long after it ended. The book gives a vivid picture of a world long since departed. The adventurers set off walking beside their horse-drawn vehicle from West Drayton, close to the present site of London Airport, passed through the centres of Maidenhead and Reading and proceeded by way of Newbury, Hungerford, Stonehenge and Salisbury to Lymington, returning by way of the New Forest, Winchester and Dorking. Suburbs, oil fumes and motor cars were unguessed hazards of the future. Curiously, because such an eccentric adventure was evidently regarded with some suspicion by those who watched them pass, they did not always find it easy to find camp sites, and milk and other supplies were harder to come by than is the case beside a modern motorway.

During her twenties my grandmother had been to Denmark with her friend Wardy (Emily Ward, who was the "Great Originator, or "G.O." of the caravan adventure) to learn about the running of nursery schools. As we discovered in my passage about the 1881 census, Mrs Ward was a pioneer of the Norland Nursery movement. Beatrice Harriet was 32 when she married in 1891. She was three years older than her husband, who had been engaged in pastoral work in Southwark; but despite her age she had seven children, the last two born when she was over 40, Barbara arriving when she was 46. Two more of our tributaries have come together; and we are left with only four great rivers crossing the plain.

CHAPTER 9. GRANDPARENTS AND PARENTS.

My grandfather, William Ingham Brooke, Rector of Barford in Warwickshire, was as much a representative of the gentry as he was a conscientious and faithful churchman. He was born in 1862 and married my grandmother, Beatrice Harriet Wallich in 1891. She had been born in Guernsey in 1859. Barford Rectory (which later became the Glebe Hotel) was a large country house beside the church, with a private gate leading from the garden into the churchyard. The Rector's and his son Oliver's graves can be seen to-day just inside the gate. In this age, when church resources are sparse and servants few and far between, the house would be regarded with horror and swiftly disposed of, but it was entirely suitable for a prosperous rector and his large family in Edwardian England. There were seven children: of those seven only one, Barbara, the youngest, was born at Barford. My mother, Grace Marjorie (weighing between 6 and 7 lbs according to Granny's record), was born at Aldeburgh on July 7th 1896. Her father was for a time Rector of the small church at Sibton, not many miles away where a branch of the family, the Acton Brookes owned (and still own) the Sibton Park estate. Nanny from Yorkshire presided over the Barford nursery, and no doubt cooked parkin and fudge for her charges as many years later she did for their children; the village boys doffed their caps to the Rector and his wife; and William Ingham, when not concerning himself with the needs of his rural parish, rode to hounds. This was a different age; and in the golden years before the First World War the elder girls went in carriages to dances in the great houses of Warwickshire, watched Oxford friends of their brother, Rupert, experiment with one of the first aeroplanes to fly in England; and were driven in the splendid cars that made their first appearance during this period and in due course replaced the carriages. One sad event marred this idyll; Oliver died of appendicitis at the age of twelve, the same complaint that so nearly killed the king and was to account for Oliver's elder brother, Rupert, in 1934. This was before the age of penicillin. A darker shadow still was to cast its gloom over the family, when so many of the young men with whom the girls had danced, and who Rupert had brought home from Oxford, went off to be killed or maimed in the War.

My grandfather clearly enjoyed the company of his children; my mother used to tell us how ruthlessly he played that game which involves counting animals seen on your side of the road in order to reach the winning total before you opponent. With the totals tied, my grandfather stopped the trap outside a cottage, hurried in and emerged triumphant with a cat to claim victory. He was bold and unlucky with his investments (though fortunately he created a trust for the benefit of his daughters). He visited Canada and invested in Vancouver property and Canadian railroads, and lost money on both; but less than he was to lose when investing in Rupert's farm just before the agricultural slump of the twenties. My mother accompanied him on a trip to South America, and when they hurried back late to their ship, anchored off the quay at Montevideo, he calmed everyone by assuring them that ships did not leave their passengers behind.

I never knew my grandfather, who died in 1923; but Granny, accompanied by the ever faithful Nanny and her sister, lived at 13 St. Peters Square in Hammersmith throughout my early childhood. Gentle, grey haired and sympathetic, she used to welcome me to her sitting room and later to her bedroom in her old age and put out the wooden bricks made by the Barford carpenter, together with the Noah's ark and the other toys from the Barford nursery. Those bricks are still played with in my nephew's house in Herefordshire as is the Barford rocking horse. Granny was charitable about the behaviour of her children in an age when standards were changing; but she never compromised her own high standards. I remember as a boy, in bed with flue, on hearing of her death, painting a card for my mother on which angels accompanied Granny to the heaven to which I was confident she would go. I also treasure the old bible that she had by her bed and which she told me that I could have when she died.

My other grandfather, William Edwards, and my grandmother Lilian, both Welsh through and through, arrived in Warwickshire from Wales in 1910, when William became Rector of Tredington where he was to remain until his retirement in 1926. Tredington is about two miles north of Shipston-on-Stour, and in those days all of it stood between the main Stratford-upon-Avon to Oxford road and the river Stour. The church is large and has an ancient history. The rectory built in 1840 had replaced a much larger mediaeval building, but was still substantial by modern standards. A photograph of the Oxford road taken in 1904 shows how much we have lost by the change from the horse drawn vehicle to the heavy lorry and the Stratford tourist bus, at least in terms of peace and beauty if not in speed and convenience, a change that began in my grandfathers time at Tredington. Even when I went to stay in the Manor Farm in 1950 with a family that had known my father and my aunt in the twenties, it was still much as it had been for centuries; and the village then would not have appeared so very different from what it had been when this sensitive Welshman arrived there in 1910.

The village history, which I bought in the church, states that Tredington in the 1920s would have looked very similar to the Tredington of 200 years earlier. Yet that cannot be quite true, because that same pamphlet contains an extract from an article written by my father for the local paper in 1919. The extract begins:

"The old people declare that many cottages have been destroyed. The tithe barn has been quite transformed, it was nearly twice the size of the present barn in the Rector's yard and possessed an open timber roof. Another large stone barn above the lower mill had lost the lichen-covered thatch that was once the admiration of every visitor, corrugated iron, that vile expedient of a niggardly age being now the popular form of roofing for all such wide surfaces. The parish stocks were placed just outside the churchyard on the north side at the end of the Manor Farm barn. Mr Potter, the Halford antiquarian, remembered them very well but towards the close of the last century, they were rooted up and used to fence in pigs".

I reproduce that piece partly because it gives a glimpse of the world in which my parents were brought up and partly because it illustrates how even then my father's writing was developing an easily recognisable style.

After his retirement my grandparents came to live on Chiswick Mall, where they were joined in 1935 just down the road by my father, mother, and their three sons. I only remember meeting him once, grey hated, and walking a terrier in Chiswick Lane just behind our house. I have a similar once seen never to be quite forgotten picture of my grandmother propped up in bed, I think with pearls around her neck, and certainly with rings on her fingers, while my Aunt Averil anxiously stands beside her, the very image of the exploited spinster daughter. Perhaps I am unfair; but I certainly always gained the impression from my mother that for much of her life my grandmother was selfish and difficult, bedridden more as a performance than a necessity. Yet it cannot be the whole story. The Rectory at Tredington was a house in which Greek and Latin were familiar tongues, the Bible an intimate friend, and a knowledge of the classics taken for granted. Sadly, I imagine that my grandfather's Welsh must have become a little rusty; there can hardly have been much use for it among the parishioners of Warwickshire. Averil, like her brother could write well and was to be the author of several books; Unlike my father, she did not go to Oxford, although her brother would never have objected to a sister who was a blue stocking. I have no knowledge of my grandmother's interests or information about her intellect; but I find it hard to believe that she did not make some positive contribution to this cultured family. I have some small, well executed watercolours, which show that she could be quite skilful with a paint brush. Like many Prichards she was strong willed and it is hard to believe that her influence was entirely negative. Yet again I find myself regretting that my parents were alive I did not ask the right questions, and now it is too late to discover the answers.

My father was born on 23rd June 1894 at Pwllywrach, the Prichard family home in Glamorgan, and his early years were spent in Wales. It was there as a boy that he must first have met my Godmother, then Nancy Hood, but later Molyneux; and it was during those years that those Welsh roots went deep: they were to draw him back again and again to stay with Glamorgan friends of his childhood; to half a century of service to the National Museum, serving on its Art Committee, Council and Court; and in due course to buy the property in the Black Mountains that is now my home. He was educated privately and at Hertford College, Oxford. He was commissioned as an officer in the First World War. I subsequently wore his Sam Brown Belt as a subaltern in the Royal Welch Fusiliers. From an early age he suffered ill-health and in particular from a duodenal ulcer and he was invalided out of the army without having served in France. As a very young man he made a lengthy pilgrimage on a bicycle to see Thomas Hardy, an early indication of his lifetime interest in poetry and literature. He took his final bar examination and later joined the editorial staff of Country Life (1921-26). He moved to the Victoria and Albert Museum, and became Keeper of the Department of Woodwork (1937-1954).

A profile that appeared in Apollo in January 1963 emphasised the importance of his scholarly work in collaboration first with Percy Macquoid and then with Margaret Jourdain in establishing correctly the roles and contributions of the major designers and manufacturers of English furniture, and correcting earlier myths. "*The two books of Mr. Edwards which helped to bring about this change were the famous Dictionary of English Furniture (with Macquoid), published 1924-1927; and the equally celebrated Georgian Cabinet makers (with Miss Jourdain), published in 1944. The demand for these two books is still so great today that they have both been re-published in recent years, and in both cases Mr Edwards, having lost his collaborators through death, has carried out a radical revision and expansion of the text single-handed. What gives the two works their popularity and authority is not only their comprehensive scope, but the fact that they are both soundly based upon documents and historical records...............their account of the furniture of the seventeenth and eighteenth centuries is accompanied by innumerable extracts and quotations from contemporary letters, memoirs and diaries: an apparatus of learning which is so skilfully employed that far from enveloping the subject in pedantic tedium, it delights the reader by leading him into the very midst of the civilisation whose daily needs these objects served. And the pleasure of the adventure is greatly increased by the eloquence of these two guides. Their prose has a balance, harmony and variety that are rare in books of this kind and tempt the reader on from one chapter to another."*

Years later they are still tempting readers and are still in demand; although the profile did not make clear that my father had completely rewritten the original three volume work, and that this version had been published in 1953. In 1963 he published a shorter, but again updated, one volume version that to-day is in even greater demand than the larger version, and a good deal easier to come by.

Margaret Jourdain was the companion of the novelist Ivy Compton Burnett. The former was large and expansive, the latter rather prim in appearance and manner; but they shared an equal passion for good food. It was rumoured that they had both subjected themselves to a Swiss treatment that enabled them to eat enormously with minimal impact on their figures. It is certainly a fact that when they were present at the annual University Boat Race party give each year on Chiswick Mall by my parents they attacked the fare provided with ruthless determination.

The profile, after reference to the seventeen years when he was Keeper of the national collection of furniture in the Victoria and Albert Museum went on *"Nor does Mr. Edwards exercise his galvanic powers upon the dead alone. He rouses the living too, sometimes a more remarkable miracle. Just as John Peel's halloo would awaken not only the dead, but the fox in the morning, so will Mr. Edwards's voice, heralding his approach in the corridor or hall, bring the somnolent to life in their dens in Bloomsbury, Bond Street, Fleet Street, Trafalgar Square or Exhibition Road. Upon hearing that vibrant clarion Mr. Edwards's acquaintances summon up their wits and prepare for a strenuous contest, well knowing that it is useless to seek refuge from this frail but dauntless man in silence, apathy or evasiveness, for he is not a man to deliver monologues, but one who revels in the thrust and parry of a lively debate between friends. His enemies would describe his conversation as provocative, while his friends who outnumber them by a hundred to one, call it an invigorating tonic. And it is indeed refreshing to hear opinions so outspoken and so well spoken; for Mr. Edwards who is one of those happy Englishmen to whom a long line of Welsh ancestors has transmitted the gift of eloquence; not merely the gift of writing, nor that of public speaking, quite common among Englishmen, but the more precious talent for private conversation. He is never tongue-tied, nor pauses to choose his words: they come promptly at his bidding, flowing forth in long classical, well-pointed sentences, redolent of Cicero and Gibbon, epigrammatic, comical, comminatory and ironical in turn. It is a pleasure to hear him ridiculing an absurd piece of pretentiousness, which he does with infectious gusto and a keen sense of the ludicrous. He is not like many scholars, irrecoverably immersed in his subject, but dismisses it from his mind as often as he comfortably can, preferring to range far and wide over all aspects of civilised life, not excluding the humbler pleasures of sport and gossip. Not even politics are barred, for Mr. Edwards is one of those rare citizens of our democracy, and one of those still rarer writers on art, who takes a lively interest in public affairs. If you see him at a private view, the centre of an animated knot of connoisseurs, the chances are that he will not be discussing the pictures on the wall, but terrifying his audience with a forecast of the disasters that will overtake the nation, if the government (or opposition) persists in its mad course. On such themes he can outdo Amos. But having got his message over, he will turn his attention to the pictures, and in that field too he is in his element, being one of the best judges of English paintings and drawings in the country"*

It was a fair picture; his interest in works of art was catholic; He would hang modern works alongside the early English water colours and drawings on his walls. Although having modest means, he acquired a considerable collection of fine English drawings and some good pieces of furniture. He was an excellent judge of artists whose reputations were not yet widely recognised as his purchases for the Contemporary Art Society for Wales show very well; and he encouraged young artists. It was he who arranged the first one man show of the works of Kyffin Williams, who in his days as a master at Highgate was a regular attendee at that most important of all events in the Edwards household, tea around about four o'clock in the afternoon. Tea was both a social event and a very necessary analgesic for someone who suffered all his life from a painful stomach disorder.

The obituary written by his old friend and publisher Denys Sutton also in Apollo after his death on the 13th December 1977, was warmly appreciative, referring to a touch of Celtic magic. He wrote; *"Ralph was a true patriot. He detested the mealy-mouthed; he stood very square in the Tory interest* [true, but he voted Labour in 1945]. *Yet it deserves to be emphasised that his conservatism was rooted in the belief--as is that of all true-blues--that compassion must be extended to the underdog; he had a proper dislike for the onward march of Corporatism and for the well-heeled Left. He was a true patrician and at his best in the old world of the landed gentry."* That last is an interesting comment; his pleasure in the company of such people arose no doubt partly from the fact that in their houses were the treasures which he loved and about which he advised them in his time at the V and A and later as Adviser to the Historic Buildings Council for England and Wales; and because they shared his own interests; but the sympathy for the underdog may well have sprung from his deeply held Christian beliefs and his knowledge of the scriptures with which he had been so familiar since childhood. Irascible he was as well; but always ready to apologise when the temper had subsided.

Denys Sutton in the same piece wrote: *"He did not bother to dwell on the past; he wanted to know what was happening now. His memories encompassed such unexpected characters as A. H. Bullen, the Shakespearian scholar and happy imbiber, and he was a close friend of Noel Carrington, the brother of Strachey's companion. There was a touch of fantasy about Ralph........"* There was no fantasy about his reviews; as Denys Sutton makes clear;" *His articles and reviews about Hogarth, Gainsborough, Reynolds and Constable were unique of their kind; literate and often trenchant, they were based on close observation. Some of his reviews were distinctly tough; Ralph never shirked from putting his opinions, but at least his victims had the consolation of being scolded in good firm prose. The Mellon Centre would perform a valuable service by bringing out a selection of his articles and reviews.*

Ralph was very much a figure of the eighteenth century; with his rakish hat and elegant cane he was rather a dandy. He could be irascible, but his friends realised that behind the mask was a man who cared about others. He was God-fearing and upright, a Britisher of the old school. His many friends came from different generations: they loved him and his wife Marjorie. He was a staunch friend, a tough adversary and a gentleman in a n age of chicanery. Dear Ralph, we shall never see your like again. He would have disagreed, for he believed in his country and its future; he always sought for truth". He was buried at Patricio just before Christmas, *1977.*

It is not surprising that the son of a Warwickshire parson should meet and marry the daughter of another; although this was no hasty affair and my father was not at first accepted. They finally married on April 15th 1926. That my mother, Marjorie Ingham Brooke, hesitated is not surprising; that he could be difficult and that his health was poor must have been obvious; and that he was impractical about domestic matters clear even when he was young. However, though not a scholar, she was widely read--and read to us as children---and she shared his interests. As a young woman she had driven ambulances in France in 1918 and repaired the punctures, eight or nine on a single journey, she used to tell us. She had a flat in London in the World's End shared with Stella Reading whose husband was to be Viceroy of India. She ran her own interior decorating business. She was the strong bedrock of a family of women, deprived by the early 1930s of their father and both brothers. Until she passed over the responsibility to my brother, Tim, she managed the affairs of The Brooke Trust and handed over the income to her sisters and their families. She coped on a relatively small income herself with the domestic affairs of her husband, three sons, a house on Chiswick Mall and a cottage in the country, the first in Suffolk, the second after 1944 in Wales. She travelled frequently with Ralph in France and Italy; and her French was fluent, and her Italian adequate. When war broke out the French onion seller with his bicycle, with whom she had frequent conversation, came to the door to say an emotional farewell, and returned in 1945 to say that he was safe. She drove a car well; but her nerve was permanently shattered teaching my father to drive! Faced by war she dealt calmly with the installation of a shelter in the house, the blitz, waiting at Paddington for sons returning from Westminster School, which had been evacuated to Bromyard in Herefordshire; and in the midst of all this she helped to run The British Restaurant in the West London Hospital.

She used a bicycle to do the shopping in Chiswick; and some time in the late forties injured her face quite badly when she fell off in St Peter's Square. From that time on she suffered acute pain all too frequently from neuralgia. Her kitchen was the despair of tidy minded people although a good deal better in that respect than her sister Faith's; but she was an excellent cook. She entertained a wide circle of friends at Suffolk House, for dinner, for those ever important teas and for large and memorable boat race parties. Despite everything she was devoted to Ralph and in every sense devoted her life to him. Having few interests except those they shared, she found the years after his death, alone in Suffolk House, difficult; and although she much enjoyed the company of her children and grandchildren, I fear that these were increasingly lonely years when her busy sons gave her inadequate time, and even the loving care of devoted friends on Chiswick Mall was not entirely adequate compensation. She died from cancer at Tim's house near Guildford on 10th September 1983.

The many little streams are now coming together in two broad valleys. We have followed the Edwards story almost to the end. I turn again to the Healings. The photograph albums that we possess convey a vivid impression of family life in the late Victorian age and the first half of this century. Members of the Healing family can be seen in the gardens of their large Tewkesbury houses, playing tennis and croquet, or on the cricket field. They can be seen on their travels in Europe. There are pictures of the mill at Tewkesbury and of weddings in the Abbey. The Healings were magistrates and churchwardens, gardeners and sportsmen, and the leading citizens of a prosperous community.

Percival L'Estrange (Paget's son and Ann's grandfather) presents a rather different and less clearly defined personality. He was educated at Sedbergh, where he won the famous ten mile run, and Queen's College, Oxford where he rowed. He was assistant master at Malvern College, where he was known as "Straggers"; and was the author of *A Progressive Course of Comparative Geography* which by 1913 had gone to six editions. *The Malvernian* records that "the simple sincerity of the man 'stuck out a yard'----and it is inconceivable that he ever had an enemy". Curiously little was said about him in the family in his later years, and a letter from his son, Guy, (quoted below) makes clear that he became a very sick man, probably suffering from shell shock as a result of war service. It was he who married Margaret McLean, creating the junction of two of our rivers, and in the happier days of his youth their children, Guy and Betty were born. Although in the period before the First World War he pioneered Alpine skiing with Arnold Lunn, this schoolmaster and author of a standard geography textbook somehow seems an odd product of a line of marcher barons and Irish landlords. It is strange, even within a family known for its reticence, particularly about matters considered delicate or embarrassing, that his grand-daughter heard little about him as a child. He was, I believe, one of the many shell shock victims of the Great War. His Scottish wife, the daughter of the Islay Far East Trader and the manse could not have been more different. Apart from anything else she loved to gamble and visit the casinos of the Riviera. She must have been brave and tough. In a letter her son Guy sent from Samarang, where he was employed by Maclaine Watson, dated 4/2/29 he wrote

"Both your last two letters contained rather bad news. The first one said that you'd heard from the doctor that father might possibly never get well, and in fact he'd rather lost hope. I did'nt quite gather from this whether he would probably pass out, or just go on as he was without regaining his senses, though both are equally bad, and rather disturbing. It must be rather trying for you". It must indeed have been trying for her and Guy's letter did not provide a great deal of comfort, but concentrated rather too much on the comfort provided by *"a couple of whiskies and sodas"* and of his Uncle Archie's drinking habits during a visit to Java. His mother's letters had revealed that his father had been certified of unsound mind. Guy thanked her for *"keeping this away from Betty and I all this time",* and added *"it does'nt seem to matter whether he's actually certified as such or not, it's merely one phase of the illness.*

Please don't worry about it, as I'm sure everyone realises it's merely a phase of neurasthenia due to the war".

In due course it was the stronger genes of both the L'Estrange and McLean families which would come out in the personalities of the two children of the union. Guy was sent to Dartmouth and a career in the Navy before joining the family business of Maclaine Watson. Betty was sent to St James's school, West Malvern. She was Head Girl and captain of tennis, lacrosse and hockey. With her father ill, she stayed frequently with her Carlisle relations at Naworth Castle in Cumberland and with the Muncasters at Muncaster Castle.

The Muncasters were L'Estrange cousins. George Burdett's younger brother, Edmund, of Twyte Lodge had married Lady Henrietta Susan Beresford. Her brother was the 9th Earl of Scarborough. Their daughter, Constance, married Lord Muncaster in 1863. (Other children of Edmund made the marriages which provide family links with Gore-Booths and Errolls. Lord Muncaster, like Paget L'Estrange, had served in the Crimea. The

Muncasters were captured, with others, by Greek brigands in 1870, when four of the party were put to death before the ransom arrived. According to Betty, the Muncasters had no children because Constance had been raped by a sepoy in India and had VD. She was never very well and spent much of her time in bed, although she lived to the good age of 78, and was buried at Muncaster in July 1917. I wonder whether it is not more likely that a Greek brigand was responsible for any rape that may have occurred. Constance would have been exceptionally unfortunate to have been both raped by a sepoy and captured by Greek brigands.

Ann's great-aunt Rhoda Ankaret L'Estrange, Paget's daughter, was therefore a first cousin of Constance Muncaster, and it was at Muncaster Castle, near Ravenglass in Cumberland, that she met Charles, Viscount Morpeth (later the 10th Earl of Carlisle) who she married there in 1894. Rhoda's mother-in-law was 'Radical Rosalind', a daughter of Lord Stanley of Alderley. Her husband, who was a good painter and keen antiquary, left the management of the estates to his wife. Teetotal as well as radical, she is alleged to have dumped the wine from the family's cellars in the lake at Castle Howard. She also arranged that Castle Howard should be left to her daughter Mary (married to Gilbert Murray) and in due course it went to Charles's younger brother, George Howard. The Carlisles were left with Naworth. During Rhoda's first pregnancy, her mother-in-law locked her up in the tower there while Charles was away. Despite these vicissitudes, she bore four children, George, Constance, Ankaret and Elizabeth. Ankaret was killed in a riding accident in 1945. She married William Jackson, on whom Ann and I called as we travelled south on the day after we became engaged. Ann remembers Rhoda well during the time when she lived in her old age with Constance at Brampton. Constance also died in an accident. Elizabeth married Lawrence Maconochie-Welwood, whose lovely garden at Kirknewton in Midlothian we inspected after a visit to the Edinburgh Festival in the late 1990s.

Betty must have had an interesting time with these unusual cousins in their grand houses in Cumberland. She was both clever and good at games; and gained a place at Somerville College, Oxford; but never took it up because her brother Guy "did not want his sister to be a bluestocking". It was a sad mistake and a decision that Betty always regretted. It is striking that it was the brother rather than the father who seems to have played the decisive role in this affair. To someone who knew them both much later in their lives, it also comes as a surprise that the strong willed Betty succumbed so easily to the advice of her brother. There was, however, no shortage of advice given or taken, as a letter dated 17/12/28 written by Guy to Betty about a possible marriage partner shows very clearly. It has a wonderful feel of the twenties, the Navy and the Far East about it, as even a few extracts will show:

"You ask my advice, but really it isn't a thing I feel competent to give my advice on. The more I learn about life the less I feel I know about it if you see what I mean. Anyway marriage is a thing to be approached with very great caution.

The first three weeks may be just the stuff, but it's the next forty years that matter.

Whoever you marry is bound to be human and have a lot of faults, but still there are a lot of very decent people in the world and especially in England.

I hope you've got no illusions left about men, and realise that there are remarkably few men over the age of say 25 who are still "He-virgins" and if they are they are probably either freaks, or practice other vices. I admit there may be one or two normal decent people who hav'nt but they are very few and far between especially in the tropics.

I must say I think it's a very good thing for a man to break out before marriage, and get it over.

I am rather doubtful if what they call "love" really exists, but maybe you know better than I do. Of course so called passion is very common. I've met plenty of women whom I would'nt at all mind sleeping with, but I'd no more think of marrying them than an Eskimo.

In spite of all this though I think the average man of our so-called class is a very good fellow, although he may break out a bit at times even when he is married to someone he likes very much and is what they call "in love with".

Another thing, I think money matters very much. It's much easier to get on together if you've enough money to avoid the smaller trials of existence and get away from each other at intervals.

Looking back on what I've written it all seems pretty good rot, as you can't really lay down the law about anything.

P.S. Whatever you do, don't marry a man from the East, or anywhere in the tropics."

Instead of Oxford, Betty trained as a dancer and became a county tennis player, touring country houses in a delightful combination of sporting and social activity. Her interest in tennis continued into old age, when it was only exceeded by her passion for racing: like her mother she loved to gamble.

On April 17th 1933 Betty wrote a short letter to Guy in pencil:

Dear Guy

Haven't written for weeks---but here is great news. Your little sister is engaged at last. About time too---I expect you'll say. Your future brother-in -law is Jim Healing. Aren't you lucky

Have suddenly realised the Air Mail is just going---so I am writing this sitting in the car with Jim outside Tewkesbury Post Office. Poor Mr Batty---won't he have a hell of a time. Anyway I feel very happy about it all. Will write you a proper letter by the next mail and tell you all about Pat's wedding which was a great show. I think the firm ought to give you leave to come and give your sister away---but I suppose that is a vain thought. No more now

Love from

Betty

Jim Healing, his brother David and sister Pat, were the children of William. J. Healing and Evelyn Gillum-Webb. Jim was educated at Wellington and Pembroke College, Cambridge, where he read economics. His father made him leave a year before his finals to go into the family business. The marriage, which was a happy one, took place at St James's, Piccadilly, on 12th June 1934. Betty's cousin, the Earl of Carlisle, who she had got to know during those visits to Cumberland as a girl, was best man. Ewan Macpherson (in a kilt of the Macpherson tartan) was a page. There were several bridesmaids; and the Reception was held at the Garden Club. Strikingly handsome and always immaculate, Jim was much less extrovert than his wife, quiet, cautious, and competent; but he shared her enthusiasm for sport. He was a keen and skilful rock climber and an enthusiastic skier. There are many photographs of Alpine holidays, with Betty frequently displaying her talents on skates as well as on skis.

At the outbreak of war in 1939 Jim joined the Gloucestershire Regiment. Because he was the eldest partner, he had to leave the army to run the Mill as flour was needed so badly. As his cousins remained soldiers this proved a heavy burden but he found time to play an active role in the Home Guard. Betty immediately joined the ATS and, because of her training as a dancer and her skill as a tennis player, became a Sgt. PT Instructor. The ATS unit then became part of the newly formed WAAF; and shortly after that Betty discovered that she was pregnant. Her Commanding Officer was not pleased. "Sergeant Healing, many of my unmarried girls are having babies; how can you, a responsible married woman have got yourself pregnant, too? No, I cannot let you have leave". Betty, despite her condition, continued her energetic activities as a PT instructor, until finally she was sent in an army lorry to Birmingham to see a gynecologist who signed her off. Ann was born in Southbank, Worcester, the first legitimate Waflet!

In the post war period Jim continued as a Director of the family business, climbed in Snowdonia, went skiing, now accompanied by his daughter as well as his wife, and grew apples and plums behind Kinsham House, their home in the Vale of Evesham. He continued to serve as a magistrate, and was Chairman of the Bench. Betty took up a new enthusiasm, politics: she was an ardent Conservative, and in due course strongly encouraged her son-in-law's political ambitions. She became a leading figure in Conservative politics in the West Midlands and served on the Executive of the National Union. She had sent her daughter to St James's (from which on one memorable occasion she ran away and hitch hiked her way home to Kinsham); and in the 1970s and 1980s she was Chairman of the Governors of the school and saw through its merger with The Abbey School.

The Healing milling business was taken over in unhappy circumstances by Associated British Foods, a firm which had used its considerable power to undermine Healings' traditional markets, making possible a successful but far from generous bid. Jim lived long enough to enjoy the company of his grand children, but then died on the banks of The Spey having landed a salmon, a good way for a fisherman to go. Betty, looking years younger than her real age, continued with undiminished energy her many activities, which included being a generous, hospitable and much loved grandmother. She died at Cheltenham Hospital in June 1991 just before her 85th birthday, remembered, as the bidding prayer at her funeral written by her granddaughter, Sophie, reminded the congregation, for her *"contribution to politics and education and, in particular, her encouragement to women in public life. A great gardener and traveller we recall her as a skier, dancer, county tennis player and, more recently a veteran archer. Often seen playing a hand of bridge or holding a race card, she knew how to turn the most difficult situation into something hilarious, and she grew old exceptionally gracefully. We remember, with love, her enormous pride in her family and her touching ability to cross the boundaries of generations. We thank God for a Granny whose gentle departure, in the fullness of age, leaves a legacy of principle, kindness and love".*

CHAPTER 10. THE RIVERS MEET.

The four rivers in the plain have come together: Brooke and Edwards, Healing and L'Estrange; and the last two now converge towards each other. I was born in Highgate on 25th February 1934, but moved with my father and mother, and two elder brothers, David and Tim, to Suffolk House, Chiswick Mall in 1935. May who was to marry Bert Hopkins, who did the garden, helped to look after me. He was a signal man on the railway, and later when I was older I visited him in his north London box and pulled the levers. I remember, on one occasion when I was about three sitting on the garden wall by the river in Chiswick and watching the rest of the family drive off in the Standard to France on holiday. May and I went off to Suffolk and there is a photograph of me there with a dog and holding a walking stick looking extremely happy. May lived to a good age in a small house in Bexley and died in 2003. I remember paying my first visit just before the war to my godmother, Nancy Molyneux, at Trewyn on the outer ridge of the Black Mountains ·in Monmouthshire, a house that I was to return to again and again in the years that followed: already Wales was calling. When war broke out I was staying in the Isle of White with J. B. Priestley. He and his first wife Jane were among my parents' oldest friends.

In the blitz we sheltered first in the cellar below the house and later in a Morrison shelter in the study. I watched the smoke from the burning docks far away to the east and blazing barges floating down the Thames from the ruins of the Cherry Blossom Shoe polish factory just up river. I was evacuated to my Aunt Margaret's house in Berkshire and then to join a Danish family called Anker-Peterson across the village green. Things got better and I came back to London, only to be driven away again by flying bombs. As the war drew to a close I was sent to Westminster Under-School and in due course to Westminster School, itself, after its return from its wartime home in Herefordshire. My brother Tim had been Head of House and Head of the Water (rowing). I was never quite so successful, but I rowed for the school, acted in a good many school and house plays (roles that included Cecily in The Importance of Being Earnest, Gertrude Queen of Denmark in Hamlet and Mark Anthony in Julius Caesar); and enjoyed myself. Two years as a soldier in the Royal Welch Fusiliers followed: once again those Welsh roots were drawing me back. I followed Tim to Trinity College, Cambridge, and there among many friends I got to know Neil Macpherson. It was to prove a friendship with significant consequences. He was the younger brother of that Ewan Macpherson who had been Jim and Betty Healing's page at their wedding. His mother was a McLean of that Islay stock whose history I have recorded. After Cambridge I worked in the City for Wm. Brandts. It was in that bastion of male exclusivity, The City Club, that I was to meet Ann. Neil Macpherson was getting married in Oban on a Tuesday, and those unable to make that journey were invited by his father to a party at the club. "Who is that girl bouncing up and down underneath the portrait of the Duke of Wellington?" I enquired. "Oh, that is Ann Healing replied Max Rendall and Gordon Macpherson together; we thought we would ask you to come and meet her for dinner later." We dined and danced at the Allegro, and so it was that the rivers met.

Ann was born on 12th June 1940. She had a deliriously happy time at school at Severn Springs, and then followed her mother to St James's, West Malvern, where she was initially less happy; she ran away; but in time she made her usual success of things and the many friends she made there have remained friends for life. There were a succession of ponies; there was hunting; dancing; and skiing: that was very much in the family tradition. She was invited by her Macpherson cousins to come and pony gillie at Attadale on the West Coast of Scotland and there discovered to her surprise that deer forests were treeless. She went up to Edinburgh to read music, a lifelong interest; but a boy friend at Cambridge and a piano teacher who was a bully prompted her to leave after a year. She worked as a secretary for Ninian Comper, the eminent church architect, and for Harold Holt, equally eminent as managers of great musicians. She was only 22 when we met. In the autumn of 1962 she returned from a holiday with an old friend in Italy and travelled north with me to Yorkshire and to Scotland. I proposed beside the Crinan canal as we came south; and we were married in Tewkesbury Abbey on the 26th of January during the bitterly cold winter of 1962-63. The many tributaries that we have traced had finally come together into a river that stills flows turbulently and strongly; but the history of that river is for others to record.

CHAPTER 11. THE DELTA.

In the last two hundred years recorded in this history the river system that we have seen growing rapidly expanded into a vast delta of cousinly relationships. In the Victorian age it was not at all unusual for there to be a dozen children or more in each generation of a single family, and a remarkably large number of them survived into adult life. As a consequence the delta is so large and its winding channels so numerous and complex that I cannot trace them individually, but can only give an impression of what it contains. The cousinly relationship is curious. Quite often close relations drift apart and first cousins only meet at weddings and funerals. Sometimes, however, we meet relations that are remote and get great pleasure from the encounters. For example, at a reception at the House of Lords I suddenly saw a badge with the name G. Ingham Brooke. "You must be a cousin I said; there are not many Ingham Brookes". It was indeed my cousin, Gavin. His grandfather, my great-uncle, was a Brigadier General who won a D.S.O. in First World War and was M.P. for Pontefract from 1925 to 1929. He had been a Trustee of the family trust set up by my grandfather. Gavin had been brought up in South Africa and was as pleased as I was to be able to re-establish family links. Or, take another case: before a visit to South Africa in 1998 a Dorset friend said you must visit my cousin, Philip Erskine, who lives near Stellenbosch. On hearing the name I said that I believed he was a cousin of mine as well, and so he was. As a result we had a lovely day in at a beautiful house with a glorious garden, and were amused to observe so many family traits repeating themselves. Our visits to the many L'Estrange relations in Ireland has been an equally fruitful source of friendship and pleasure; and conversations with Petra Coffey and Winston Guthrie Jones led to my growing interest in this branch of the family and in due course to the production of this record. There are pilgrimages that simply have to be made. Members of the Edwards family at some time or other feel an urge to visit Hendrefelen, that farm in north Cardigan from which we all sprang. On my first visit as a boy Cousin Joseph, with perfect courtesy put his jacket round my mother's shoulders to protect her from the rain; and, waiving his arm expansively towards the steep hill behind the farm, said "As far as the eye can see the land is mine". The truth was that we could not see very far; but felt a shared sense of family pride. Ann enjoys a similar sense of coming home on visits to the Island of Islay.

A tour through the delta resembles a journey down the history of the British Empire. The cousins scattered far and wide. Of the twelve children of Colonel Henry Peisley L'Estrange, the elder brother of George Burdett, three died in India, one was lost at sea, and one died in Fiji. One of George Burdett's daughters, Ann's great-great aunt, Emily Mary, married Sir Henry Waldermar Lawrence, the son of Lawrence of Lucknow, the great Victorian hero, killed during the Indian Mutiny of 1857. He was the first white baby born in Nepal (in1845). His grandson, Sir John Lawrence, author, expert on Russia, and President of the Society for Study of Religion and Communism celebrated his 90th birthday in 1998, and died a few years later..

Another grandchild of George Burdett, Violet (the daughter of his second son Champagné) married Annan Bryce, Far East merchant, Home Rule supporter and MP for Inverness Burghs (1906-18) who created a great garden on Garnish Island in Bantry Bay, bequeathed to the Irish nation by his son Roland. Violet was arrested in 1920 to stop her speaking out against actions by the army. The Irish Republic takes equal pride in another L'Estrange connection, Constance Gore-Booth, Countess Markievitz, although my mother in law used to remark "she brought shame on the family"! Constances's brother Sir Josslyn Gore-Booth, owner of Lissadel, a great Irish House, was married to Mary L'Estrange, the grand daughter of George Burdett's younger brother Edmund. Constance was second-in-command of one of the Rebel garrisons during the Easter Rising. She was court-martialled and sentenced to death, but reprieved on account of her sex. She was elected the first British woman M.P. but never took her seat, and when she died in 1927, three hundred thousand people lined the streets for her funeral, and eight lorries were needed just to carry the flowers. Despite any "shame on the family" Ann and I earned immense, if undeserved, credit from a party of Irish school children when Ann claimed that she was a relation while standing in the prison cell she had occupied in Dublin.

An equally famous, or perhaps I should say notorious cousin, was Jocelyn, 22nd Earl of Erroll, murdered in Happy Valley in Kenya. George Burdett's niece Mary had married the 20th Earl. The 24th Earl who sits with me in the Lords is a hard working businessman and a model of respectability. Rather more unusual is the present Earl of Carlisle whose great-grandmother Rhoda Ankaret was Ann's great-aunt. He is a Liberal Democrat and has an obsession about the Baltic States where he now lives, having lost his seat in the House of Lords as a result of the Blairite revolution of 1999. There are more distant L'Estrange cousins who live in South Africa and the United States and who take a keen interest in the family history.

A Brooke family gathering held in August 2000 at Armitage Bridge Mills to celebrate the millennium makes it possible for me to bring the history of the firm up to date and to record much of what had happened to the family since we last heard about them at the end of the 19th century. As the century ended the colonies provided new markets. (The first Australian wool had been bought as far back as 1849). However the scale of operations demanded fresh capital, and John Brooke and Sons became a limited company in 1895. As in Napoleonic times war proved profitable; and the company benefited from the sale of uniforms in both the Boer War and the Great War. The thirties were to prove much more difficult, with losses made in every year from 1930 to 1939. Edward Brooke took over the management in 1938 and saved the business, helped again by war. Among the products produced between 1939 and 1945 were cloth for service uniforms and cloth impregnated with rubber which was wrapped round the petrol tanks of Lancaster bombers. With the return of peace the company extended its range into materials for women's clothes and was a supplier to Marks and Spencer.

When the Marks and Spencer contract was cancelled in 1978 the writing was on the wall: and Edward and his sons, Massimo and Mark, wisely began the company's withdrawal from manufacturing, finally ceasing production of the last products in 1988, four hundred and forty seven years after John Brooke began it all in the reign of Henry VIII. Massimo and Mark then energetically undertook the task of finding new uses for the mill, some of the buildings of which are listed as of architectural or historic importance. John Brooke and Sons moved into the new millennium as the Yorkshire Technology and Office Park with about thirty businesses on a site that now includes a splendid art gallery in the North Light Building, a television studio, and schools for art and dancing.

Among those who gathered on that August Bank Holiday weekend in the North Light Building were representatives of the Acton and Kendall Brookes of Sibton Park (where my Grandfather had been Rector as a young man). Many of them had been born and brought up in southern Africa, but they also included a professor from Pittsburg, Pennsylvania. There was a direct descendant of the Anne Brooke who, in the early 19th century, had turned down a proposal from Benjamin Ingham and then married Charles Brook. There were numerous descendants of William Brooke and Gertrude Ingham, the branch that carried the business into the modern era, central among them Massimo and Mark, together with Massimo's daughters and his American son-in-law. Their first cousin, Sophie, was there, as was her one year old grandson, Caspar, not the only child from the 18th generation. Sophie is the daughter of Humphrey Brooke who contributed to my school fees at a moment of family financial crisis and was Secretary of the Royal Academy. He married the Countess Nathalie Benckendorff, the daughter of the last Imperial Russian Ambassador to the Court of St James's. Massimo and Mark told us of the history of the firm and family, and took us to worship in the church at Holme which had been largely built and decorated by means of Brooke money.

Ingham Brookes were strongly represented. The contingent included William Bennett a professor of music and distinguished flautist, a retired surgeon, a doctor, a psychiatrist, an academic scientist, a distinguished gardener, a *Times* leader writer, a former Cabinet Minister, a broadcaster, two businessmen, and my first cousin, Anne, from Canada, perhaps best described as a brave adventurer. Only in one respect would our Victorian forebears have been surprised and disappointed by the occupations of their descendants, and that would have been by the absence of any clergy in that list.

Charles Weston Brooke, who for some years had worked with Massimo and Mark in the mill, was the leading representative of the Weston Brookes. Like his great-grandmother before him he had married a member of the Weston family, Tanya. The Weston connection with our family had begun when Charles Samuel Weston of the Bengal Army married Elizabeth Godby, the elder sister of my great-grandmother, Grace, and father of Charles's great-grandmother, Blanche. Charles's elder brother, Sir Alistair Weston Brooke, Bt, after farming in Herefordshire for some years, now lives in Llandrindod Wells in Powys. That may or may not have something to do with the fact that his wife, Susan, is Welsh; but for a Scot, born and brought up near Bonar Bridge in north-east Scotland, it also seems to suggest a certain restlessness of spirit, although nothing like that of his great-uncle, John Weston Brooke, who was killed in China looking for the source of the Bramaputra. There was also a strong contingent at the gathering who are the offspring of Charles's great-aunt Dorothy Law and are my third cousins.

Also present was a great-great granddaughter of the Edward Brooke of Field House who had undergone a conversion and become a Baptist Minister. She was able to fill a yawning gap in my version of the family tree, although we still know much less about Edward's descendants than we do about other parts of the family. The links with a good many of these cousins are distant; but that proved no discouragement to some trans-Atlantic visitors that August day for whom the initials above the door of Exchange House in Holme of William Brooke and Sarah Kaye were just as evocative as reminders of past history as they were for the rest of us. William and Sarah's daughter, Lydia, who died in 1761 married a Robert Walker who died in 1794. From these two descend numberless Canadian relations: Waddington, Frink. Reynolds. Wienard, Foster, Oland, Scolfield, Morton, Zed, Prichard, Harries are all names in that roll-call. The late Elizabeth Frink, distinguished sculptor and painter, thus proves to have been a cousin as well.

A short time after typing the sentence about my Law relations it occurred to me that if they were Brooke cousins they must also be Godby cousins; and that apart from Blanche, I had not given thought to the offspring of my great-grandmother Grace's brothers and sisters. Brother Robert had died in the Indian Mutiny. Brother Christopher, a Major-General, had married, so there may be relations with the name of Godby. Sister Louisa married a Fergusson and so Fegussons must be added to the fast growing list of connections. Indeed I have a letter of congratulations written by a Fergusson to my grandfather on his engagement. Blanch, too, had brothers and sisters who married and had children, so that I may well have second cousins called Weston, Nash, Allen and Bulmer, all names that appear in the Godby and van Rhenen family tree. Just as those original tiny rivulets emerged from the marshes to join and form larger tributaries, so in the present century an ever growing number of streams spread out and lose themselves in the Delta. Some time after the Millennium reunion Mark Brooke married and, happily, another male Brooke has been born to carry the line forward into yet another generation.

The Edwards family produced an extraordinary number of Welsh clergy; but also soldiers and colonial administrators. Brigadier Graham Thomas George Edwards who was born in 1864 commanded the 20th Hussars; General Sir George Erskine gave distinguished service in the last war and after; and Sir Gerald Kennedy Trevaskis was High Commissioner for Aden. Both Edwards and Prichard cousins served in The Royal Welch Fusiliers. They included my father's first cousins David Prichard and Hubert de Burgh Prichard, the latter killed in Normandy in 1944. His son, Mathew, has given distinguished service of another kind to Wales as Chairman of The Welsh Arts Council and President of The National Museums and Galleries. My cousin Michael Edwards, grandson of The Archbishop, spent most of the war as a prisoner in Germany and was C.O. of the Regimental Depot at Wrexham when I joined the Regiment as a National Serviceman. Michael's brother James was my son Rupert's headmaster at Heatherdown; and I have also met some of the children and grandchildren of the three other brothers.

We maintain contact with the quite numerous Healing cousins, among them, members of the Rollin and Robertson families. Peter Healing and his wife Elizabeth created an outstanding garden at Kemmerton in Worcestershire. Their son, Julian, was a partner of my brother Tim, in the stockbrokers, Grieveson Grant, and after finishing his career as a director of Kleinwort Benson has retired with his French wife to a beautiful house in France. David Rollin has lived all his working life in Argentina where there is now a growing colony of Rollin offspring, and his brother Jerry lives in the Philippines. Ann's Scottish cousins, whose genesis we researched on the island of Islay and whose fortunes were made in Far East trade seem to have become less adventurous in subsequent generations, but those who settled back in Scotland provide generous hospitality and the excuse to revisit the Highlands. Among those cousins are McLeans, Macphersons, Fraser-Mackenzies, Maconochie-Welwoods and Ballingals.

My children and grandchildren, together with my numerous nephews and nieces and their offspring, are also adding to the current. The river flows on and the channels of the delta multiply. Looking back to the past the story is full of fascination. No doubt endless surprises lie in the future; and perhaps, one day my grandchildren will explore further into the delta.

ILLUSTRATIONS

1) Sir Thomas L'Estrange, by Hans Holbein the younger.
2) Nathaniel Wallich, Vice-President of the Linnean Society (portrait in the Society premises, Burlington House).
3) Brooke family:
   a) Captain Leonard Collings(Father-in-law of Nathaniel Wallich)
   b) Beatrice Brooke (neé Wallich)
   c) The Rev. William Ingham Brooke
   d) Marjorie Brooke (1918)
4) McLean family:
   a) Mrs Lachlan McLean (neé Elizabeth Cameron) and May, Margaret, Lucy & Nora
   b) Mrs Lachlan McLean
   c) Margaret L'Estrange (neé McLean).
   d) Percival l'Estrange
5) Betty Healing (neé L'Estrange)
6) Healing family:
   a) Mrs Frederick H. Healing (neé Gillum-Webb) and Jim, David and Pat
   b) Frederick Henry Healing
   c) Jim and Betty Healing (neé L'Estrange)
   d) Ankaret Healing
7) Edwards family:
   a) Ralph Edwards
   b) Marjorie Edwards
   c) Nicholas Edwards
   d) Ralph and Marjorie Edwards
8) Edwards and Healing families 26 January 1963
9) Nick and Ann Edwards 26 January 1963

APPENDIX

THE McLEAN AND McNEILL FAMILY
INVOLVEMENT IN
MACLAINE WATSON AND CO
IN JAVA AND THE FAR EAST
(* IN THE TEXT INDICATE FOOTNOTES)

Gillian Maclaine, son of Allan Maclaine of Scalcastle on the island of Mull, was born in 1798. He originally went to Java in 1820 to work for the London East India House of D & P Machlachlan. It is clear from his letters* that Messrs Maclachlan did not intend him to set up in business in Java, but had arranged that he should go on to Calcutta to join McIntyre & Co, their associated House there, as a salaried employee. They were furious when he remained in Java and set up as a coffee planter in the Princely States. As he had no capital of his own it was a bold move and for a time his financial position was precarious. He would have made about £250 on a consignment of opium which he sold soon after his arrival in Batavia in 1820 (purchased with money that had been lent him by his uncle); but soon his uncle was demanding repayment. In 1821 he was lent 40,000 florins by the Dutch administration and he "gained an exceptionally good character with the Dutch officials, who placed him above all the other British, and quite in a class by himself" *, but the costs of the coffee plantation venture were still more than the resources he had to cover them. Relations with Machlachlans and with McIntyre & Co were to some extent restored in 1822 when, after a visit by McIntyre, Gillian Maclaine & Co was set up and the coffee plantations were taken into joint ownership. Although the new partnership included Gillian himself it is clear that a hard bargain had been struck, and there now began a long period of very strained relations with his new partners. He wrote to his uncle in February 1826 *"their conduct towards me has, I confess, been far from liberal........you must not be surprised if you hear shortly of my having separated from them, for I cannot afford to toil longer in this climate, without a sufficient recompense for my labour"*. As we shall see, he did separate from them; but the debts he had with Machlachlans continued to dog him until 1832 when he finalised a settlement with their assignees (the firm having by then gone bankrupt). His financial problems during this period must have been made much worse by the turmoil in central Java caused by the Java War 1825-1830.

That these were unsettled times is, perhaps, indicated by the fact that in 1828 he sold a house that he had built at a cost of £20,000 in 1827.

The separation referred to in the letter to his uncle took place in 1827 when the firm of G. Maclaine and Co was dissolved by mutual consent of the partners, and Gillian Maclaine and Edward Watson (who is also said to have been lent money by a relative) pooled their resources to found Maclaine Watson to do business in the colonial capital Batavia (the present day Jakarta). Gillian's own letters provide proof that Edward Watson (who was a Londoner, educated at Christ's Hospital) had not travelled out with him to Java in 1820 and that they had not known each other in London as one history claims. Edward Watson probably arrived in Java in 1821; and on arriving back in Batavia from his coffee plantation in 1822 Gillian found him a "most able assistant". Edward Watson was fortunate not to have been a partner with the Machlachlans (or it would appear so committed to costly ventures), and thus avoided the financial problems that Gillian suffered in those years. In a letter written in 1832 Gillian said "*Watson, who fortunately for him was not a partner in the bad years of the old concern, I find now actually rich-while I who made him a partner from being my clerk, am obliged to begin the work again*". Watson, who married in 1835, retired and returned home in 1836.

On the same day in 1827 that Maclaine Watson was founded the associated firm of McNeill & Co, with a John McNeill as the active partner, was also established in Samarang*. Some time before that Alexander Colin McLean, ship owner and ship's captain (born on Islay in 1796), had also arrived in Java. We do not know whether he met Gillian Maclaine for the first time while he was there, or whether he came to Java as a result of contacts that had been made in Scotland. There is a family legend that while in Java he was asked to deliver a bale of cloth to the McNeill family at Ardnacross on the Kintyre peninsular, and that while he was there he met Margaret McNeill who married in 1828 soon after his return. However, Margaret's father, Neil, had been born at Kidalton on Islay and she herself was born on the island, so it seems likely that the two families would have known each other long before Alexander Colin sailed to the Far East. There is a third possibility, and that is that it was Margaret's brother John 5th of Ardnacross (born on Islay in 1800) who was responsible for the introduction.

Having given myself the task of writing this history, I was immediately confronted with a question: who was the John McNeill* of McNeill & Co in Samarang? I had seen no evidence that John 5th of Ardnacross went to Java, but it seemed unlikely that an entirely different family of McNeills than those who later played such a central role were briefly involved in the business only to disappear from the scene completely. I knew that Alexander Colin Maclean's brother-in-law, Alexander McNeill (born in 1813), did go to Java, and that he worked in Samarang and became a partner in the firm. Could the founder of McNeill and Co have been his elder brother, John 5th of Ardnacross, born in 1800 on Islay, who was later (like his brother) to marry a daughter of William Loudon*. It seemed to me possible that John had sailed with his McLean neighbour to Java and remained there to establish the Samarang branch in which his younger brother Alexander later worked. Professor G. Roger Knight at the University of Adelaide, a leading historian of the sugar industry in Java, gave me the answer to my question in the form of a McNeill (spelt MacNeill) family tree, written in Dutch obtained from a friend in The Hague! This confirmed that my speculation had been in large part correct. John had arrived in the Dutch East Indies as early as 1819. He was indeed a founding partner of McNeill and Co. He was a merchant and recorded as living in Surabaya (Dutch: Soerabaja) in 1824-5, in Samarang from 1826 to 1837 and in Batavia 1841-1844. The Dutch document does not record where he was during the interval between 1837 and 1841, and it does not tell us what took him to Java in the first place. Did he go there with Alexander Colin McLean or did he get there first? We know that Alexander Colin was back in Islay before 1828 when he married Margaret McNeill. We also know that he was in command of a Dutch vessel in Batavia as early as 1819, but not when he first arrived in the Far East (see footnote, page 137). The Dutch document provides clear evidence that John McNeill 5th of Ardnacross was the founding partner of McNeill & Co and worked with Gillian Maclaine at the very start of the enterprise in 1827. It also proves that he actually arrived in Java before him.

A vivid account of events in Java at the time of the Java War can be found in Donald Maclaine Campbell's *Java Past and Present*, published in 1915 (two years after the death of the author, who had been a partner in Maclaine Watson). From this marvellous book we learn that a John McNeill (or MacNeill) had been agent for Gillian Maclaine & Co in Surabaya as early as 1823 and had taken part in the fighting that led to the death of a number of Europeans then living in the town. It must surely have been the same John McNeill. We also learn that, years later, in 1840, he bought the house that Gillian had built and sold in the 1820s and lived in it until 1843. If Donald Maclaine Campbell had lived to write the third volume that he had planned we would have learned a great deal more about the history of Maclaine Watson and its partners. There are footnotes that tantalisingly refer to a text that was never to appear*.

In 1830, Gillian Maclaine made a return voyage to Europe, probably in an effort to restore his health after a serious illness. While there he took the opportunity to obtain financial and commercial support for his firm; and as we know he visited Scotland it seems highly probable that he took the opportunity to renew his previous contact with Alexander Colin McLean. It seems equally probable that he met Alexander McNeill, the ship captain's seventeen year old brother-in-law who was the younger brother of John McNeill in Samarang. We don't know exactly what happened, but we do know that Alexander McNeill went to Java in 1832, where he married or lived with someone called Sienok. There were two children by that marriage, both born in Java, and the son Richard will appear in the story later. Gillian Maclaine, before returning to Java, went to Holland where he renewed his contacts with a number of prominent and influential Dutch acquaintances, such as H.G. Baron Nahuijs van Burgst (a major figure in Dutch colonial circles in the 1820s and 1830s), who he had first met in the Princely States. He left Rotterdam in February 1832 on the Dutch ship Anthony. Among the passengers was the eighteen year old Catherina van Beusechen, accompanied by her family, who he married soon after his arrival in Batavia in May of the same year. Also on board was a young Arthur Fraser, who surely must have been the same Arthur Fraser who was to be a founder of the firm Fraser Eaton and Co. in Surabaya in 1835.

At this point it is convenient to explain the relationship between the three companies. A pamphlet entitled *THE FIRST ONE HUNDRED YEARS 1827-1927 MACLAINE WATSON & CO. McNEILL & CO. FRASER EATON AND CO.*, written by an employee (Tony Leland) in 1927, gives an account of the history of the firms and explains their relationship. It also provides a list of all the partners during those first one hundred years. The pamphlet explains that "The three firms are sister firms, and a partner in one is also a partner in the other two. The majority of the partners are resident in Java, but a certain number, varying usually from one to three, are resident elsewhere. This applies to the working partners, in addition to whom are non-active partners who maintain a financial interest in the three firms. For a number of years" (this is 1927) "the three firms have been represented in London by Messrs. Maclaine & Co., 14 Fenchurch Street, E.C., who have acted as their agents. Messrs. Maclaine & Co. have this year, for purposes of internal administration, converted themselves into a private limited company, entitled Maclaine Watson & Co, Ltd.".

The early 1830s, the time when Gillean Maclaine returned to Java, was a critical period in the development of the colonial economy in the island which was emerging as a major producer of cane sugar. In 1834 there were 22 European manufacturers working under Government contract who processed the harvests of half the area farmed under the colonial cultivation system. Chinese sugar workers handled the other half. After 1837 the Chinese were increasingly excluded and by 1840 more than 100 contracts had been issued. The Europeans were also beginning to introduce new engines, new engineers and new methods, a process which developed rapidly over the next two decades and which transformed the industry. According to one history*, "Until the 1850s the consortium of Fraser, Eaton & Co (Surabaya), Maclaine and Watson (Batavia) and McNeill (Semarang) were second only to the NHM (*Nederlandsche Handel-Maatschappis*) in terms of economic muscle and as suppliers of capital to the sugar industry". It was not just sugar that the firms traded in. They acted as agents for the import of cotton and other manufactured goods from the UK and India and for exports from Java, as well as representing the major shipping lines. Partners served on the boards of the Java Bank and of shipping companies. They also became directly involved in production. As early as 1827 Maclaine Watson held "two estates Malambong and Coeripan (sic) both of considerable value". They were land owners, sugar traders and agricultural bankers.

Things must have gone well for Gillean Maclaine in the 1830s, and in December 1838 he bought land in Hope Valley in Australia with the object of establishing a sheep farm there. He wrote to his brother Angus, who was a Church of Scotland Minister in Inverary, inviting him to come out and manage the farm. Angus accepted; but while he was on his way to Australia, Gillian decided to return to Scotland with his whole family and they were all drowned at sea in a hurricane somewhere between Mauritius and the Cape of Good Hope in 1840. It was a tragic end to a remarkable life and career, but it was not to be the end of the business.

Alexander McNeill must, by then, been playing a major role in the affairs of the company, and he continued to do so until he returned to Scotland in 1850 where he married his second wife, Isabella Maria Loudon, the daughter of William Loudon (or Louden). His first wife (assuming that they were actually married) may have died as many young wives did at that time from a tropical illness or in childbirth. Perhaps the more interesting question is what led to the Loudon marriage. It is a question made even more interesting because of the fact that Alexander's brother, John 5th of Ardnacross, married Isabella's sister Agnes five years later. William Loudon* was born in 1782 in Tannadice, Angus. He served as a Commander in the Royal Navy, and became agent and Factor to Lord Elphinstone on his Carberry Tower estates at Inveresk in Midlothian. The 1841 Scotland Census records (under the name Louden) that he and his family were then living at Inveresk. William's brother was Alexander Loudon, wrongly recorded in some histories as a Scottish Army Captain. He had been a Midshipman in the Royal Navy and he came to Java with Raffles. He was the father of James Loudon, Governor-General Netherlands East Indies, 1871-1884, who was created Jonkheer in the peerage of the Netherlands in 1874, the progenitor of a well known Dutch family. Alexander Loudon held a sugar contract together with an indigo contract in 1830 and he obtained a second sugar contract near Samarang in 1832. He became a naturalized Netherlands subject in 1824. The Governor-General was Alexander's 4th son. His eldest son was Hugh Hope Loudon who became a tea planter in Java, served in the Netherlands East Indies Civil Service and as a City Councillor in The Hague. Hugh Hope Loudon was the father of James Hope Loudon who was a Partner in Maclaine Watson from 1903 to 1917. Marriage to the influential Loudons must have been of considerable assistance in strengthening the McNeill and McLean business interests. William Loudon's wife, Elizabeth Webster, was born in 1806, her brother William in 1801, and their daughters, Isabella and Agnes, who were both to marry McNeills, in 1826 and 1827. They were all in the same house in Inveresk at the time of the 1841 census.

The 1850s was the decade in which the McLeans began to play an equal part with the McNeills in the management of the firm. Alexander McNeill's nephew, Lachlan McLean (born in 1830), the elder son and second child of Alexander Colin McLean, must have gone out to Java at about the time that his uncle returned to Scotland and marriage; and he was followed by his younger brother, Neil (born 1836) a few years later. Lachlan was a partner in Maclaine Watson from 1860 to 1879 and Neil from 1871 to 1879. Lachlan returned from Java in 1868, married Elizabeth Cameron, and rented Islay House from the Morrison family. He renewed the lease in 1878, but two years later died of appendicitis. Neil married his first cousin Elizabeth, a daughter of Alexander McNeill in 1871, the same year in which he became a partner. On his retirement, Neil settled at Breda, Near Alford, in Aberdeenshire.

Elizabeth's brothers, Neil McNeill and William Loudon McNeill also joined the firm. Neil was a partner from 1882 until 1917. William Loudon McNeill who married Anna van Devalaar in Java in 1879 was a partner from 1891 until 1917, and was senior partner for part of that time. Their brother, Alexander, born in 1862, is shown on one family record as having worked in the firm, but he is not included in the list of partners. Another brother, Richard, the product of Alexander McNeill's first marriage, who was born in Java in 1842 and who married in Java Wilhelmina Joanna Couperus, was a partner from 1885 to 1906 and played a particularly crucial role in ensuring the survival of the firm during the crisis years 1883 to 1885. He died in Holland in 1915.

In those years 1883-1885 intense depression in consuming markets forced the price of sugar down below the cost of production and kept it there. Those who had brought sugar saw it depreciate in value, whilst in the case of the three firms, the situation was very seriously aggravated by the urgent and recurring necessity of providing funds for the numerous mills financed by them under contract arrangements. The years of the sugar crisis were further complicated by the incidence of heavy attacks of leaf disease in the gardens of many coffee plantations, especially in mid Java. For three consecutive years the business made considerable losses; but it survived. During this period its destiny lay in the hands of Neil McNeill and Richard McNeill in Java and G. H. Miesegaes and A. P. Cameron in London. Because this paper is about the McNeills and McLeans, it neglects the contribution of the other partners, of whom the two Miesegaes, were notable examples, G. H. Miesegaes being a partner from 1860 until his death in 1913 and A. F. Miesegaes from 1897 to 1920; and also neglected the part played by other employees, some of whom completed more than fifty years service.

During the Great War (1914-1918), as a result of the reduction in the output of European beet sugar, Java sugar was shipped to England in large quantities. The firm was commissioned by the British Government to ship the quantities required, and for this service it received the thanks of The Royal Commission on the Sugar Supply.

We have seen that two generations of McNeills and McLeans had tied the families together by marrying cousins, and the practice was to be repeated in the third generation when Isabella McNeill, a daughter of William Loudon McNeill and Anna van Devalaar, married Colin McLean, eldest son of Neil who had settled at Breda. A great deal of the family information contained in this paper has been provided by one of their grandsons, Neil Macpherson. Colin, who was born in Batavia, became a regular soldier and was killed in the great war, but his brother Neil Gillean McLean did join the firm, made a fortune in Java, and was a partner from 1913 to 1921. Their brother Loudon Neil McLean became a partner in 1917. Their cousin, A.C. Ballingal (Alexander), the son of Neil MacLean's sister Annabella was a partner 1912 to 1921, when he returned to the United Kingdom. His son, Niel* Cameron (known as Peter), maintained the Ballingal contribution right up to 1960. His widow, Kathleen, tells me that he became a partner in 1947 and remained in the firm until 1960 when they went to Africa. Isabella's brother Neil McNeill Jr, born in Java in 1885, became a partner in 1917, while their sister Flora, as a widow, married Gourlay Macindoe, who was also to play an important role.

On leaving Fettes, Gourlay Macindoe had entered the Glasgow office of Ker, Bolton and Co. In 1911 he sailed to Java, but in 1915 he returned to Europe to fight in the war and was seriously injured in 1917. With the war ended, he returned to Ker, Bolton & Co in Java; but then accepted an offer to join Maclaine Watson & Co, became a partner in 1926 and later becoming chairman. His niece wrote "*We came to know of his life, colleagues and friends because he wrote to his father, if not weekly, then fortnightly, often sending photographs.----- In 1931, at the age of 40, he returned to the London office of Maclaine Watson & Co to join his brother-in-lawn Neil McNeill and various relations of Flora. That year the UK abandoned the gold standard, and the interest rate on 5% War Loan was cut to 3.5%.-----The 1939/45 war created problems for Maclaine, Watson&Co when Java was occupied by the Japanese and Holland, where much business was done, was occupied by the Germans. However, despite the intensive bomb damage to the City of London the offices at 14 Fenchurch Street survived. After the war there were further problems as the Dutch relinquished Java resulting for a time in a communist regime. Things did gradually sort themselves out and, in due course, Gourlay and Flora visited Java. However, the nature of the business had altered fundamentally and the firm had to diversify its activities-in some cases unsuccessfully-and Gourlay had great worries up to his death".*

Richard McNeill's sons (he had six children all born in Java) may also have worked for the firm. Two died in Holland and the third went to Australia.

I have jumped far ahead following the fortunes of the McNeills and Macindoes in the firm. In the meantime the descendants of Alexander Colin's eldest son, Lachlan McLean, had been playing their part. His grandsons, Ken and Charles Howard joined the firm in the 1920s and worked in Samarang alongside their first cousin (and Ann's uncle) Guy L'Estrange. Colin McLean (of Breda)'s son Callum also worked with them (and was imprisoned by the Japanese during the second world war). Guy's letters home home between 1928 and 1935 tell us more about the social life of the partners than their business, but mention the Chairman J.G.D.R. Cruden, who became a partner in 1926. A generation earlier a wild party involving Alexander Ballingal and his cronies finished with the old club house in Samarang in flames. The partners paid for its reconstruction.* Donald Campbell tells us in *Java:Past & Present* that there was "a very good club at Samarang called the "Harmonie" built in 1909. This must have been the club rebuilt after the fire. Guy, after war service in the Navy, was to return to Indonesia after the war as British Consul in Makassar. Many of the partners had for well over a century acted as consuls or vice-consuls. Charles Howard was British vice-consul in the Celebes at the outbreak of war in 1939. He was a close friend of the German vice-consul. They discussed the looming conflict and dined together the night before they returned to Europe to fight for their respective countries. They were never to see each other again.

The last member of the family to join the firm may have been Michael McNeill, the grandson of Alexander McNeill of Shennaton, who was a brother of the Isabella who married Colin McLean and who was born in Java.

The Indonesian branch of the company seems to have been put out of business in the chaotic period between the failed coup attempt in 1965 and Soekarno's final replacement by Soeharto in 1968. In 1965 the troubles were so severe that all the British residents were forced to withdraw to Singapore. They returned for a short time; but then the 17th century head office of the company was burned down and the company's properties were seized. Ivor Stanard and Roy Bennett continued the business in Singapore until the Singapore branch was acquired by Ralli International, part of the Bowater Group, some time in the 1970s. Ralli International, a commodity trading company, had been acquired by Bowater in 1973 in a deal masterminded by Jim Slater the previous year. In 1981 Cargill Inc, a large commodity trading company purchased the cotton, fibre and rubber trading interests of the Bowater Corporation for a reported $27m. The acquisition included the Ralli Group and Maclaine Watson of Singapore.

Another company, Swire and Maclaine, a joint venture between Butterfield and Swire and Maclaine Watson had been formed in 1946. It represented the culmination of a long relationship between the two organizations. Since 1886 sugar from Indonesia supplied by Maclaine Watson had been refined by Swire in Hong Kong, and marketed under the brand Taikoo (Taikoo being Swire's "hong" name). Butterfield and Swire became Maclaine Watson's China agent and Maclaine Watson was agent for The China Navigation Company (Swire's deep-sea shipping arm) in Batavia, Makassar, Samarang and Surabaya. I am grateful to Nicolas Maclean of Pennycross CMG, for providing me with the history of Swire and Maclaine, much of it based on a note in the company's Minute Book, which records that at the end of the war, John Swire & Sons decided to try their hands at merchanting, in order to replace the income lost to them by the destruction of the sugar refinery in Hong Kong, and to find work for non-shipping staff. On the reopening of the Hong Kong office towards the end of 1945 the merchant department got off to a brisk and profitable start. Early in 1946 John Swire & Sons were approached by Maclaine Watson & Co., 14 Fenchurch Street, who said that they were anxious to enter the general merchant business in China and Japan, and they proposed that a 50/50 company might be formed for the purpose, with both companies having equal shares. Shortly before the war Maclaine Watson had bought a controlling interest in a small merchant firm, Pentreath & Co, in Hong Kong, which had dealt mainly in sugar. Pentreath and Co and its two active partners were given a 3% share in the new company. Initially, Swire and Maclaine, which was incorporated on 17 July 1946, dealt in everything from steel to frozen meat, alcohol and bicycles. Swire and Maclaine seems to have become a wholly-owned subsidiary of Butterfield and Swire in 1956, though it only really took off when Lydia Dunn (now Baroness Dunn) was running it. It obtained the franchise for Reedbock, which Swire still has. The company was still going strong at the time of the 50th anniversary in 1996, though the trading activities encompassed by Swire and Maclaine are now conducted by

Swire Resources, which principally markets sports gear. Swire and Maclaine was sold to Li & Fung in May 2000.

Maclaine Watson and Co Ltd in London was acquired by Drexel Burnham Lambert Holdings in 1979, presumably at the time of the disposal of the Singapore company. The Pension Ombudsman in London determined a case involving the pension of one of the London staff in 1993. The name of the company can be found in the law books and on the web in cases arising from the collapse of the International Tin Council. In one case brought by the Department of Trade and Industry an important point of international law was established.

It would appear that in different ways and under different ownership the Singapore and London branches continued in existence until the last quarter of the 20th century, a fact that might have surprised Gillian Maclaine when he founded the company in 1827 and when he set out on his last fateful voyage in 1840.

Notes:

- There is a problem about spelling. The McNeills varied the spelling of the name. The Loudons are recorded in the 1851 census as Loudens; and within the company Semerang is usually called Samarang (it was by Ann's Uncle Guy in all his letters). The Ballingals spell the Christian name Niel with the i before the e "due to a Christening error generations ago".
- G. Roger Knight is engaged in transcribing, editing and annotating several batches of Gillian Maclaine's letters. The information that he has sent me (including quotations from the letters) provides clear evidence that Edward Watson (a Londoner, educated at Christ's Hospital) did not sail with Gillian Maclaine to Java in 1820 and that they did not meet before they were in Java. The story that they had worked together in London and arrived together in Java quoted in *The First One Hundred Years* is clearly incorrect. The Dutch "Registers of European Population" have Edward arriving in Java/Batavia in 1821.
- The story about the club house fire in Samarang was told by an old employee to Kathleen Ballingal.
- The introduction to *Java: Past & Present* tells us that when Campbell died in 1913 "the first part of the book was written, that is the portion presented in these two volumes. Whether the material he left for the second part, the commercial section-will be published later in a third

volume has yet to be decided". It is hardly surprising, that in the middle of the Great War the material remained unpublished.

References:

The Cultivation System (1830-1870) and its private entrepreneurs on colonial Java. Ulbe Bosma.

Sugarlandia Revisited. Sugar and Colonialism in Asia and the Americas, 1800-1940. Ulbe Bosma, Juan Giusti-Cordero and G. Roger Knight Adelaide University.

Dr J. B. Loudon of Cowbridge, Glamorgan spent a great deal of time and energy researching the Loudons, and he sent a copy of his "Descendants of John Loudon c1690-c1750" to Neil Macpherson (c 1995).

Java: Past & Present. A Description of The Most Beautiful Country in The World by Donald Maclaine Campbell published in London by William Heinemann, 1915.

Alexander Colin McLean
Footnote

While still proof reading I was given copies of letters that prove that Alexander Colin McLean was commanding a Dutch vessel in Batavia in 1819. He commanded other Dutch ships in the Far East before 1825 when he purchased his own vessel. He named her the Loch Indaal. In 1827 he appears to have sold her for 25,000 guilders, making a loss due to "the miserable state of The Colonial Trade" and "the opening of the ports to foreign ships". The money was placed with G Maclaine & Co. and in August 1827 "2 boxes of treasure" were shipped to his account with John McNeill in Samarang". James Loudon told a cousin of McLean in South Africa that he was acquainted with him and would forward any correspondence. There is a letter to McLean dated 4 December 1827 c/o Maclaine Watson & Co. about his decision to return home, and on 13 December 1827 Gillian Maclaine signed letters commending "my good friend Mr Colin Maclean (*sic*)". The letters prove that Alexander Colin McLean was involved with Gillian Maclaine, John McNeill, and James Loudon during the years when the business of Maclaine Watson was being established.

I have talked to Michael McNeill of Shennaton, who worked for the firm in the 1970s where he was involved in commodity trading in the Metal Exchange. His office was in Mincing Lane, and he was told that the nearby

Fenchurch Street office was destroyed in the Blitz. He said that unwise investments were made in those last years. He knew Peter Ballingal who had by then returned from abroad to the London office.